The Beatles!

The Inside Story Behind the World's Greatest Rock and Roll Band

By Kerry Kensington

with a Foreword
by Neil Young

Special Library Edition

Library House Books
www.libraryhousebooks.com
Paramount, CA.

Library of Congress Cataloging-in-Publication

The Beatles! The Inside Story Behind the
World's Greatest Rock and Roll Band
Kerry Kensington
with a Foreword by Neil Young
Special Library Edition

ISBN: 978-1-936828-61-6 (Softcover)

First Collector's Edition 2018

CONTENTS

FOREWORD BY NEIL YOUNG 4

PROLOGUE: THE FIRST COMING OF THE BEATLES 6

JOHN LENNON'S CHILDHOOD... 16

PAUL McCARTNEY'S CHILDHOOD 23

GEORGE HARRISON'S CHILDHOOD...................................... 29

JOHN, PAUL, GEORGE AND PETE: LEARNING THE TRADE.. 34

HAMBURG AND THE MAKING OF A GROUP 41

BRIAN EPSTEIN BECOMES THE BEATLES' MANAGER 49

RINGO STARR'S CHILDHOOD 56

INSTANT FAME OR, THE ROYAL COMMAND PERFORMANCE
.... 64

TOURING ENGLAND AND THE FALL OF PARIS..................... 75

UNDERSTANDING THE BEATLEMANIACS............................. 84

HARD DAY'S NIGHT AND AN EASY TOUR 91

TOURING GREAT BRITAIN AND FILMING *HELP!* 101

WHAT ARE THE BEATLES REALLY LIKE? 114

THEY RECEIVE THE ORDER OF THE BRITISH EMPIRE AND
MEET ELVIS PRESLEY 124

JOHN AND JESUS AND AN END TO TOURING 135

THE CHANGING PATTERN OF BEATLE SOUND 149

THEY WANT TO TURN US ON: A MUSICAL MATURATION 155

TRANSCENDENTAL MEDITATION AND THE MAGICAL
MYSTERY TOUR 162

THE FUTURE STRETCHES OUT... 170

INDEX 178

FOREWORD BY NEIL YOUNG

The Beatles emergence in the early 60's, and their timely collaborations with agent/manager Brian Epstein and Parlophone producer, George Martin is a remarkable sequence of events. More remarkable is that the four members of the band, John Lennon, Paul McCartney, George Harrison, and Ringo Starr found each other at all, much less form the first band to create an astonishing international following within a few short months. And, it was hardly a following, it was more like mass hysteria or as it was proclaimed by the press — 'BEALTLEMANIA'. Their influence went far beyond the musical. The two movies A HARD DAY'S NIGHT and HELP, also the animated YELLOW SUBMARINE, were enormous successes which were really, extended music videos by present day definitions. They also made 'music videos' (short films, really) which often did not merely document a performance, but would interpret the song visually and had far reaching influences to the present day. Some of the videos were animated in the style of the pop artist of Peter Max, perhaps the most famous of the psychedelic artists of the late 60's and 70's. The fashion world was certainly eager to catch the coattails of the Beatles. Men's hair began to lengthen in the mid 60's, and clothing stores could not keep the British Mod or Carnaby Street style on the racks for more than a day. Rock and Roll culture was birthed by Elvis and the gang from the 50's but had little effect beyond the USA except for a small minority in England The new Pop-Culture, which grew apace with the career of the Beatles engulfed the world. The Beatles were popular throughout Asia, Europe, and the Americas. Their touring career was a 'sold out' arena rock situation which has been enjoyed by many bands since, but they were the first to pack out these enormous venues, city after city. The world simply gave it up for the Beatles. Rock/Pop music was never the same; a music not rock and roll, something related to, but also separate from, which inspired thousands of young men and women to pick up the guitar, learn three chords and start writing songs. The Beatles were made, by the crown, Distinguished Members of the British Empire—an honor never before bestowed on musicians. Paul went on to be made a Peer of the Realm—Lord Paul, as it were. In my opinion, the wellspring of their inspiration was their unique chemistry. They only began to experience problems in the late 60's when the inevitable problems presented by 3 (of four) staggeringly talented song writers began to feel the need to go in their own directions. Many point to Yoko Ono as the demon who destroyed the group. Certainly, her influence over John was resented by the other members of the band, but the group had run its course in many ways and their legacy of albums and enormous hit song catalogue completely vindicates their decisions to say 'we've done this, and we're moving on to individual projects.

The Beatle's success inspired an atmosphere of experimentation. Their innovations which made them sound 'different' were now in the ears of young musicians everywhere. This did not create a generation of Beatles Tribute bands, or clones, but more importantly sparked the imagination of thousands of would-be song writers and rock stars. The idea that old, well-trodden paths of song writing were sacred, was no longer a stifling, restrictive road map to music making. Progressive Rock, Art Rock, Hard Rock, Punk, Glam Rock, Heavy Metal, Country Rock, etc., et al, are just a few of the new lines of Rock which sprang up in the 70's and in the wake of The Beatles. The idea of what a song could be had changed dramatically, and this infusion of experimentation has been the most invigorating aspect and lasting influence of The Beatles legacy.

PROLOGUE: THE FIRST COMING OF THE BEATLES

FEBRUARY, 1964

On Friday, February 7, 1964, the U.S.A. foresaw another crisis with Cuba: Fidel Castro had cut off the Guantanamo water supply. Balancing this crisis. President Johnson promised water aid to Israel, pledging atomic power as well, while making a bid to the Soviet Union to join a ban on nuclear arms.

London and Paris agreed to build a rail tunnel under the English Channel, an almost dreamlike feat of engineering while in Jackson, Mississippi, the case against the accused killer of black civil rights leader Medgar Evers went to an all-white jury.

In fashions, the Paris Spring Look was in, and the decision was that the ideal woman for the spring ahead would be "soft, feminine, and young, but not a giddy teenager." Skirt hems were kept primly at the kneecap.

And that same day, at Kennedy International Airport in Queens, New York, 3,000 teenagers stood four deep in the upper arcade of the International Arrivals Building to give a screaming, hysterical welcome to four English boys. Airport officials termed the reception "Incredible. We've never seen anything like this before, not even for kings and queens!" But the reception was hardly surprising to anyone in the "know." These four were kings and the kingdom they ruled was larger, geographically, than any other on earth. But until February 7th, it was a vast distance away from all adults; the age differential had kept the great majority of them ignorant of the fact that such a kingdom even existed.

Screaming and chanting "We want the Beatles," the crowd of youngsters, mostly girls, started the coronation process that was to crown the four shaggy heads.

The process was furthered that night by massive crowds of young people storming police barricades at the Hotel Plaza where the four Beatles had a ten-room suite and a guard on twenty-four-hour duty.

The Beatles had left the airport in true royal fashion, his own Cadillac limousine, while the 200 reporters and photographers for magazines, newspapers, and foreign publications tried to make some sense out of the bedlam left behind.

Right at the start, in the Arrivals Building, the pattern was set and the beginning of a legend was created. One reporter called out, "Will you sing for us?"

Beatle John Lennon snapped back, "We need money first."

"How do you account for your success?" was countered with, "We have a press agent."

As quick on the uptake as Lennon, Ringo Starr answered "What do you think of Beethoven?" with, "I love him—especially his poems."

"We have a message for you." Paul McCartney beamed at the group, and into the waiting silence ordered, "Buy more Beatles records."

They swept off to the city, and the girls streamed after them by bus and taxi and private car. "That hair! They're so different, not like American singers. American singers are so clean-cut."

And yet it was a clean-cut attitude beneath the surface appearance of long hair and tight pants that pulled the teenagers in. It was a clean cutting-away of all dross and surface nonsense, a cutting right to the core of matters, that endeared them. They had a message, sure. "Buy more Beatles records. We sing for money." As blatant as that, and as honest.

The teenagers responded to the honesty, crowned the hairy heads, camped outside the Plaza day and night, and set the boys up as full-fledged teenage idols.

The adults, who are always slow to accept reality, shook their heads in bewilderment and, not understanding the why or wherefore of the whole phenomenon, promptly began to put the four boys down. Jack Gould, the New York Times television reviewer, saw them that Sunday night on the Ed Sullivan show, and received not even a fragment of the message.

"A business-like appearance," he said. "The boys hardly did for daughter what Elvis Presley did for her older sister and Frank Sinatra for mother."

He sniped on, calling them "Conservative conformists" and he attributed to them a "bemused awareness that they might qualify as the world's highest paid recreation directors." He concluded that Beatlemania was "a fine mass placebo."

In another adult attempt to handle the problem, reviewer Theodore Strongin became pseudo-serious, and wrote, "The Beatles have a tendency to build phrases around unresolved leading tones. This precipitates the ear into a false modal frame that temporarily turns the fifth of the scale into the tonic, momentarily suggesting die Mixylydian mode."

To show he wasn't really taking them that seriously, and could "put on" as well as die Beatles, he described their voices as "hoarsely incoherent," and ventured to suggest die longer parents objected to them, the "longer the child will squeal so hysterically."

This was the reaction to the appearance of the Beatles on Ed Sullivan's Sunday night show. Three days later they gave their Carnegie Hall concert. The three days were hectic ones, at least for die Beatle fans. On the day of the concert, Lincoln's Birthday, about a dozen young girls were injured in die mounting hysteria that accompanied the constant demonstrations wherever the Beatles showed up. Fortunately the injuries were limited to cuts and bruises.

Shoes, clothes, schoolbooks—all were torn or ripped from the girls as they eddied around in wild, howling glee at the Plaza Hotel, Perm Station, and Carnegie Hall. Mounted patrolmen tried to keep order at the Plaza, but the huge square in front of the hotel was like a juvenile battlefield. At one point die army of youngsters charged die police blockade, tore down the flag the police were using to mark their headquarters, and snapped it in two.

In the heat of the excitement; the police, furious at the fact that they could barely handle the children without roughing them up, and knowing full well the bad publicity such roughing-up would bring (these were nice middle-class. youngsters, no left-wing demonstrators), accused the press agents of bringing in the fans by the busload.

An unfair accusation, undoubtedly, for if Brian Epstein, the Beatles' manager, told the truth, there was never any need for press agents or publicity build-ups. "My secretary and I coped as best we could," Mr. Epstein said, "with the indescribable volume of interest which poured into the hotel by cable, telephone, and personal report." He went on to express his complete disbelief at what was happening.

The excitement and wild adulation of the young crowd probably helped restore some of the Beatles' sense of ego. This had been badly damaged during their brief trip to Washington, D.C., on the Tuesday after the Ed Sullivan show. They went to perform there for an audience of 8,000, and attended a reception by Ambassador Sir David Ormsby-Gore, who later became Lord Hariech.

Lord and Lady Hariech, whether they meant to or not, had filled the reception with upper-class British com-patriots. There are some conflicting stories about what actually happened, but Brian Epstein claimed one guest was ill-mannered enough to cut off a lock of Ringo's hair while the other Beatles were ordered, quite peremptorily, to sign a vast number of autograph books.

It was foolish treatment to offer the young men who prided themselves on their proletarian backgrounds. They left the embassy party in a huff, defensively aware of the contempt the English upper class always seems to have for any of the lower classes who make good.

The return to New York by train must have helped restore their bruised egos. As the train pulled in that after-noon, 1,500 young fans swept past police barriers and stormed the train.

Spirited off the train beforehand, and taken to the street level in an elevator used "for visiting royalty" the singers still didn't escape their loyal subjects. It's doubtful whether they really wanted to. Like all good monarchs they recognized the value of a rousing demonstration, and admitted good-naturedly that their job was to dodge bodily harm.

As night descended on the city, there were even anti-Beatle demonstrations. A group of seventy-five young men, torn by the loss of their sweethearts to the British singers, picketed across the street from Carnegie Hall that night, carrying anti-Beatle signs. A near riot, sparked by an angry attack of loyal girl fans, was narrowly averted by the police.

The concert itself was a roaring success, as every other Beatle concert in America has been, and it completely eradicated the sour taste of the embassy party.

Few reports of the concert were able to analyze the music. Evidently the audience reaction was so overwhelming that very little singing penetrated the high sonic boom of the fans.

During the first two selections, the audience kept up a sustained falsetto baying. At the third number Paul McCartney figuratively threw in the sponge and asked the audience to join in and clap and stamp their feet. It's a credit to the architects who designed Carnegie Hall that the building is still standing.

Rows of girls screamed, bounced up and down, and waved madly. Because one of the Beatles once told an interviewer that he could never get enough "jelly babies," or jelly beans as they're called in America, the jelly bean had become a symbol with Beatle fans. The fifth number was drowned out by the patter of jelly beans hurled by the audience.

By the seventh number, things were getting a bit sticky, even for the understanding four. John Lennon put laughter aside and screamed at the audience, "Shut up!"

They loved it all, and screamed back, even louder. Banners inscribed with "I love Paul" were unfurled when McCartney tried to sing a ballad.

All in all, it was an exhausting, cathartic evening for the fans, 2,900 of them for the first concert and 2,900 for the second, with an outside mob impossible to estimate.

It was, however, a triumphant evening for the Beatles. Back in their suite on the twelfth floor of the Plaza Hotel they were deluged by telegrams and boxes of fan mail.

"We get 12,000 letters a day," Ringo estimated, and John Lennon solemnly said, "What's more, we're going to answer every one of them . . . personally."

That night while their two road managers, Neil Aspinall and Malcolm Stevens, carefully signed the Beatles' names to piles of photographs for the fans, and room service kept delivering Scotch, ice and cokes, the four boys relaxed in the confident knowledge that they had successfully conquered America. If the teenage mobs were any indication, America was ready to give the country back to the British.

In the days that followed, the mobs of fans remained true. Whenever the Beatles left the hotel, as they frequently did to dine at "21", twist at the Peppermint Lounge, or tease the bunnies at the Playboy Club, the fans roared and surged through the police barricades, fainted and shrieked and threw hair rollers and jelly beans, sometimes not even taking the candy out of the bags.

When the four arrived at Miami for the second Sullivan show taping, the South rallied to their cause with its own brand of southern-fried ballyhoo, producing a chimpanzee, a gaggle, of bathing beauties and 8,000 teenagers at the airport.

At the hotel, Ringo pulled a young, pretty girl into the elevator with him just as the doors closed. Later, almost frantically, the reporters crowded around and asked him, "Who was she?"

"Just a bird I know," Ringo answered airily.

"What's her last name?"

"Haven't a clue. Don't know her that well," Ringo snapped back.

The wildness, the humor, the sense of jubilation grew in Miami. The Beatles spent time on a yacht, swam in a private pool, and visited Cassius Clay at his training camp.

Back at Kennedy Airport, the four British boys were not forgotten. As they changed planes to wing off to England, another breathless mob of thousands of teenagers waited for hours to see them hurry from one plane to the other. Five girls collapsed and the mob screamed again and again and again. The curious mechanism that creates such turnouts is never spontaneous but almost always reflects a great deal of undercover dealing. A clue to just why the Beatles craze hit the teenagers of America and stayed with them lies in a rather prim statement of Brian Epstein, who in telling about this first Beatle visit to America said, "The DJs [disk jockeys] had a good time, but within a few days I had to stop it very severely."

What he was referring to was the unqualified endorsements the Beatles gave over the radio. They had no hesitation in recommending a disk jockey's show or product. "It's the greatest. Listen to this show, listen to that one." Their approvals were taped and used on the air as endorsements by the disk jockeys.

What they were doing, Epstein felt, was promoting commercial enterprises without reward, discernment, or discrimination, in short, without a kickback. Epstein felt that they were "taken in" by the disk jockeys.

The four boys, however, were really head and shoulders above their manager, or had a clearer vision. Early on, they recognized that the entire spectacle of their descent on America, the wild ovation at Kennedy Airport, the storming of the barricades at the Plaza, the twelve girls who hid in their bathtub, the four who dressed up as maids to get a glimpse of them, the two who spent forty-eight hours in a broom closet, all of it was a direct result of the months of determined and careful build-up by American disk jockeys before they ever arrived.

It is very likely that Epstein, even though he professed amazement at the free publicity given the disk jockeys by the Beatles, was also aware that the disk jockeys were responsible for the Beatles' American success. However, Epstein always appeared a bit uneasy about his own role in the Beatles' success, and he was not secure enough to give others the credit due to them.

The Beatles themselves knew how much die disk jockeys had done and they were satisfied. When they left, it was with the disk jockeys' promise that just because the Beatles were so good in endorsing and confirming without qualification, they in turn would keep up the output and activity on the Beatles' behalf.

When "Can't Buy Me Love," their fifth record, was released in America, the disk jockeys were as good as their word. Their promise materialized, and the record slipped at once into the number one popularity groove.

By the time they were ready to return to England, by the time all the dust had settled, certain factors became clear. As far as publicity was concerned, the newspapers conceded that little more than a week in America had made them "undisputed titans of American popular music." But they added, with proper adult scorn, that the Beatles' "high-yield, low-security eminence" may yet cause them to become the "vocal scourge" of the entire western world.

Agreeing with a general feeling that this kind of popularity did not just "happen," the newspapers went on to explain the artful contrivance that brought it all about.

The taking of America by storm would not have been possible, they said, if the Beatles had not first taken England by storm. England has a far lesser density of rock-'n'-roll stars than America. It was no great problem, the analytical pundits of journalism decided, for the Beatles to become number one in England. After that, all they had to do was follow their fame across the Atlantic.

Then another reviewer, brushing the whole thing off casually, predicted that they faced an awful prospect of demise. They are a craze, he said hopefully, and since a craze is a form of inflation, it may precede a crash.

As to publicity, he noted that the novelty, popularity and excitement of crazes must be constantly renewed. New exploits must in fact be manufactured.

As they left our shores back in February, 1964, the Beatles had the satisfaction of knowing that they were number one in publications such as Billboard, Cash Box, Variety, Music Vendor, and others, where a year before they were hardly known. Obviously, if the newspaper evaluation of their popularity was correct, they had been carefully created, they had not sprung full-grown from music's brow. But how had they been created?

A press interview with Brian Epstein allowed him to take some of the credit. "When I first saw them," he told a press conference, "I saw four boys with little stage presentation. They had scrubby haircuts and scrubby clothes, black jackets, and jeans." (In truth the jeans were leather and the total picture was less of scrubbiness than of a sort of brutal animal vitality. As one London teenage girl put it, "They came on tough, sort of made your legs turn to water.")

"I recognized the appeal of their beat," Epstein continued, "and I rather liked their humor. Through it all came a quality of personal presence and personality that seemed to be full of possibilities. I got friendly with them and became their manager."

The build-up in England, Epstein explained, was very much his own doing. "I shouted from the rooftops. They thought I was mad, but I went on shouting."

However, when the noise died down it turned out that the significant shouting had been done not so much by Mr. Epstein as by British teenagers. The kids discovered the Beatles at the Cavern in Liverpool, followed them to the London Palladium, endured them at a Royal Command Performance, and shouted continually whenever they appeared, even, it turned out, at airports.

Ed Sullivan, who keeps his finger on the pulse of the world's teenage frenzies, heard the shouting himself when he was at London Airport. He decided that the shouting was very much of the same caliber as that which had ballooned Elvis Presley to fame, and after some bargaining with Epstein, who fought for top billing rather than top payment, he signed the Beatles for three performances.

It's interesting that almost a month before the Sullivan show the Beatles appeared on a taped section of the Jack Paar show, a television first that went virtually unnoticed. The Beatles were not in the country then. The tape had been made in Britain, and their own peculiarly magnetic presence was not available to attract the hordes of young people.

A story in Life magazine a week before the boys arrived here may also have had a considerable amount to do with their popularity. It was headlined, "Four Screaming Mopheads Break Up England: Here Come Those Beatles."

But again, looking back on the wreckage of the Beatles' first visit, it seems likely that the disk jockeys of America were the most important factor in the Beatles' American success.

But how did it all reach the disk jockeys? It is hardly possible, by any stretch of the imagination, that they all, with no preconceived planning, broke the news of the new group at the same time to a breathless teenage world.

No group ever concurs, as America's disk jockeys did, without tremendous behind-the-scenes planning and work, and the work was indeed done, and by the force that had the most to' gain from the Beatles' success, by Capitol Records, the company that released the Beatles' disks in America.

Capitol had rushed its Beatle releases to the trade to match the wave of publicity that they were sure would result from their first American visit. Then Capitol Records had ensured that publicity by sending out a million copies of a four-page paper crammed with Beatle publicity to all disk jockeys, buyers, and the press. They also supplied the disk jockeys with recordings of a number of Beatle songs and an "open-end" interview with the four boys themselves.

This open-end interview was a most clever device arranged to allow the disk jockeys to ask questions which could be matched to the prerecorded answers. Played in the studio, with the disk jockey filling in the blanks, it gave the illusion that each disk jockey was conducting a private interview. A code allowed them to vary the questions, but ask the proper ones to make sense out of the prerecorded answers.

Radio, Capitol records knew, was what really sold records, and this handy device helped give the Beatles tremendous coverage on the air.

The disk jockeys pushing the Beatle records, also set up the vast fan turnout for the Beatle appearances.

These were the overt efforts of Capitol Records. Less acceptable methods may have been used to guarantee screaming attendance at their concerts. There were accusations against Capitol Records of calls to local high schools with offers of money for the Student Aid Fund to help rouse interest, and of money offered the fans to go into Carnegie Hall and carry on. But these accusations were quickly put down, Capitol insisting that such tricks were not needed. Even if the accusations were true, there was an incredible chain reaction to the entire visit. One thing sparked another, and Beatlemania grew and grew.

There was also the economic angle of the entire visit. Manufacturers jumped on the wagon very quickly, and by the time the Beatles had left our shores in 1964 there were at least sixty quiet legal suits against misuse of the Beatle name. By then there were Beatle shirts, slacks, hats, pajamas, and even wigs. An approved agency, Seltaeb (Beatles spelled backwards), was set up by an independent group, with Epstein's approval, and gleeful predictions were made of a projected earning of at least 50 million dollars in Beatle projects during the coming year.

Beatle motor scooters and even Beatle cars were considered, but the real money was to lie in Beatle clothing. The Reliance Manufacturing Company, which obtained from Epstein the sole American license to turn out Beatle products, stated that even though they had gone in-to it with a tongue-in-cheek attitude, it had, before the Beatles had even left our shores, mushroomed into the biggest promotion in the company's sixty years of business with retail sales of more than 2.5 million dollars.

Besides clothing, there were toys, and, let's not forget, wigs. There were 15,000 Beatle wigs a day turned out by the time the original four mopheads had flown back home.

The adult world, which had scoffed at their music and at the demonstrations, now proceeded to cash in on their teenage popularity. Beatlemania was big business.

JOHN LENNON'S CHILDHOOD

1940 TO 1956:

Reputed to have more fog than London, Liverpool has been described as a burnt-out planet, deserted by all its inhabitants. The very name for the people who live there, Liverpudlians, is ugly. It does away with the "pool" and all its connotations of forest glades, cleanliness, and fun, and it substitutes "puddle," muddy, ugly, and unwanted.

Until very recently the only thing in Liverpool worth visiting was the new Roman Catholic cathedral, planned to compete with St. Peter's in Rome and St. John the Divine in New York as one of the three largest cathedrals in the world. But even this bid for greatness has come off a poor second, or indeed third. Most travelers describe the new cathedral as funereal and remote, with none of the warmth of Christianity. Nothing in it stands out distinctly, the colors in the stained glass windows are jumbled, and the acoustics are God-awful.

Three miles from the sea, Liverpool spreads for eight and one half miles along the right bank of the River Mersey. It is the second seaport in the British Commonwealth, and the fourth largest city in Great Britain, with a population close to one million.

Before 1963, guidebooks to Britain gave Liverpool one tired paragraph, evidently despairing of any tourists. In spite of its uncertain tourist attractions, the city was felt to' be architecturally unsurpassed by any other in Great Britain. It has its share of libraries, art galleries, museums, parks, public gardens, and recreation areas. It has two municipal golf courses, five boating lakes, seventy bowling greens, and an open-air theater, to say nothing of six cemeteries and a crematorium.

Liverpool is about two hundred miles northwest of London, but it received some very heavy bombing during World War II. In one week, in 1941, 1,453 people were killed and 1,065 injured; during the war 120,000 homes were destroyed or damaged.

Educationally the city is reputed to have an efficient system, and it has a good reputation for its work among the physically and mentally handicapped. Every student of promise, the city proclaims proudly, is assured of adequate financial assistance in attending a university.

Besides being a port city with heavy trade and shipping, Liverpool is a large and growing industrial center. Historically, it dates from 1207, when King John issued its first charter; but it wasn't until 1715, when the first dock was completed, that the city really began to grow and develop. Trade with the New World made it what it is today.

It is interesting to find that there is a very large Irish quarter in Liverpool, and traditionally the Irish of Liverpool have been looked down on by the British. J. B. Priestley, the novelist, toured the Liverpool of the era when the Beatles were born, and said of the Irish in the city, "There are a very large number of them in Liverpool, and though I suppose there was a time when the city encouraged them to settle in it, probably to supply cheap labor, I imagine Liverpool would be glad to be rid of them now."

The four Beatles are all of Irish extraction, all products of this Liverpool background, all probably exposed as children to this anti-Irish bias. Bias, all too often, has strong effects in the formative years, sometimes destructive, but also, in many cases, strengthening. This is particularly true when the childhood is not too smooth. While two of the four Beatles had apparently normal childhoods, one came from a broken home and one lost a parent in his teens.

John Winston Lennon is usually considered the leader of the Beatles. Certainly he speaks for the rest, is the most articulate of the four, and probably the one with the most claim to being an intellectual, for what that is worth He himself denies this and tends, like the rest, to favor the image of untutored, semiliterate, working-class boys

Even while speaking as their leader, he frequently denies the need for leadership. "We're a group," he told an early interviewer. "We've always been a group. Not any one of us worked any harder than the others. We've always done what we had to do together. Of course every once m a while, we'll notice that the way the act is going one or another of us isn't getting enough play. The minute we realize this, we shuffle things around so it's breaking out even. That way everyone's doing an equal share and everyone's getting an equal share."

This disclaimer to leadership may be true, but Paul

McCartney has gone on record as saying, "John is our leader. He's the chief Beatle."

There is logic to this because, in a sense, John has been the most cohesive force in the group. Though three months younger than Ringo, he seems a good deal older than the others, a good deal more settled, and

17

there is no denying that John started the group.

John was born in 1940, on October 9th, in Liverpool Maternity Hospital. According to the record, he was named John after his paternal grandfather and Winston in honor of Churchill.

His father, Alfred Lennon, was hardly the steadiest of men, and his mother, Julia Stanley, seems to have been no great prop to lean on. The marriage met with deep disapproval from Julia's parents, who appear to have been wise to take such a stand. Alfred, or Fred, was one of Liverpool's merchant seamen, and he was off on a voyage before the wedding rice had settled. Julia was a movie theater attendant, an usherette, at Liverpool's Trocadero Theatre. Though the groom was twenty-six and the bride twenty-four, neither apparently was mature enough to make a go of the marriage.

John was born while his father was off at sea. Julia received payments from her husband for some eighteen months after that, and then Fred Lennon disappeared. Julia took her loss lightly, and went on to another man, and the child was shuffled off to one of Julia's four sisters, Mum Smith and her husband George. The family had disapproved of Fred from the beginning, and his disappearance confirmed their unfavorable opinion, but they helped out with the child. Life with his aunt assumed a pleasant enough pattern tor John, except for occasional tormented tuggings from either his father, home from the sea and ready to take the child off to live with him, or his mother tied up with another man and ready to "provide a home for her baby. The tuggings were evidently stabilized by the aunt, who seems to have been both generous and good-hearted. To the boy, however, his mother represented fun, good humor, and approval.

Lennon himself, a number of times, has said that he had a happy childhood, a life of uninterrupted calm and a wonderful mother-" An early friend of his, Nigel Whalley, recalls Julia Lennon in the same vein "one of the happiest women I have ever known. Always full of fun. She encouraged John to take up music and chivvied him on.

The memory of the smiling, encouraging mother is but one created out of sentimentality and public relations. As full of fun as she may have been, she left the real work of raising the boy to the aunt. And, if all the evidence is carefully examined, young John probably had an unhappy childhood. In freer moments, he has described himself as a bad kid,

18

always in trouble, always "acting up." In school, he felt his teachers not only didn't understand him, but were actually indifferent.

How these contradictions jibe is quite simple. The biographical material given to casual interviewers and fan magazines is usually spun out of whole cloth to fit editorial requirements. When the subject is as prone to wisecracks" and "put-ons" as John Lennon, winnowing the truth from the gags becomes almost impossible

John attended school at Liverpool's Dovedale Primary and here there is some objective evidence of his stay; the biggest impression he made on the school was his initials deeply carved in the lavatory door. '

His friends from that time, his schoolmates and neighbors, while admitting that the dazzle of his later fame this is just what he needed to develop as a performer, for above all he states that she approved of his music at a time when his aunt considered it nothing but a waste of time.

While Pete Shotten recalled John as wild and reckless, a teacher in one of his art classes had a different view, or saw a different aspect of the boy. "John was very reticent and quiet," he said. "His work wasn't good, but then neither was that of the other students. It was hardly a school with a high academic rating."

This teacher goes on to recall that John's friends were very sympathetic toward him and helped cover up his mistakes. In contrast to Pete Shotten's opinion and the opinion of John's aunt, this teacher says, "I don't remember him as a leader. His friend Stuart Sutcliff was the group's trend-setter."

He did remember John playing the guitar, but added, "He rehearsed mainly at school because his aunt wouldn't allow him to play it at home. He was always told, 'pack up that guitar and get down to work.' "

This fits in with the serious approach of his aunt, the idea that music was simply "fooling around" and that his only hope of a trade to carry him through life lay in art. It's a pleasant bit of irony, and though his aunt seems to have forgotten it, many neighbors and friends still recall her attitude.

Asked how he felt about John, the teacher admitted that as a child he liked him. Was this another rosy memory, or had he really been fond of the boy?

"I really was fond of him. I liked him because I go for people who are different."

When pressed about John's art, he said that while at first he didn't think John had any unusual talent, he changed his mind when he saw his sketchbook filled with satirical drawings and comments about the faculty and students.

"They were good, perhaps even brilliant in their perspicacity though not in their draughtsmanship," the teacher said. "They showed me a brand new Lennon. They showed that the boy could think."

John's drawings were evidently accepted with delight by the entire faculty, even those who were lampooned in the sketchbook. This, John's first taste of acceptance by the Establishment, seemed to provide all the impetus he needed to improve his general work and move ahead in a field he enjoyed.

There is something a little sad in this, in the discovery that it may all boil down to a simple cliché, that in acceptance there is strength. The ability to be what John is today, a world leader in music, may all stem from the Establishment's unqualified acceptance of that music. It is doubly sad when you consider that these boys are symbols of rebellion against the Establishment.

John's art talent, though not exceptional, was promising enough to get him a recommendation to the Graphic School of Art. At first they refused him because of his delinquency, but finally, after much persuasion from the Quarry Bank School, they accepted him. However, he wasn't accepted in graphic arts, the field he was best in, but in painting, an area in which he was lost.

"Painting was not his strong point. Graphic art was, and after six months his art future faded away and he left the school." This was his teacher's view. What actually happened was that music gained an edge as the boy be" came more involved in it, and finally art lost out.

Cynthia Powell, two years younger than John, was a student in the same art school. Later she became his wife, but at the time, according to one of his teachers, she helped a great deal in keeping him in school and studying.

"Even though she was top girl in her class, she always managed to spare time for John. Even in those days they were made for each other."

During his days at Quarry Bank School, when he was thirteen, Aunt Mimi's husband, George Smith, died of cirrhosis of the liver. In retrospect, John's affection for his uncle seems to have been more for his aunt's benefit. His aunt was evidently hard pressed to make ends meet, even boarding students toward the end of her husband's life.

Julia, who had come back on the scene now with another man, became a more accepting figure to John than his aunt. At home he was constantly urged to do better work at school, to forget his music. On the other hand, whatever he did was all right with Julia. Her careless acceptance, however, didn't last long. When he was fourteen, she was killed in an auto accident.

Nigel Whalley, John's close friend, saw the accident happen. He and John, who was staying at Julia's at the time, planned to go out together. Nigel had come to call for him and while knocking at the door he heard a scream of brakes. "I turned and saw someone flying up in the air. It was John's mother. When I got there, she was just lying in the road, not moving. It was horrible."

Julia had been hit by a car driven by an off-duty policeman, and she died in the ambulance on the way to the hospital.

John took her death very hard, possibly because he felt he was just getting to know her, and possibly because her death seemed a final abandonment.

Nigel tells a strange story of John's attempt to exorcise her spirit. One evening after her death he invited a group of his friends to Julia's house and, seating them round a circular table, told them they were going to hold a seance. He turned down the lights, spread lettered cards around the table, medium fashion, and began to rotate his hand around a glass tumbler.

The tumbler moved and spelled out a series of senseless words, while John sat calm and aloof. "To this day," Nigel reports, "I don't know if there was a spirit there that night or if John was just having us on."

This same year "Rock Around the Clock," the theme song from The Blackboard Jungle, a motion picture about juvenile delinquency in the American school system, hit England with smashing reverberations. It was rock 'n' roll with a vengeance, a bold, hard sexual beat that eventually became the very pattern for the Liverpool sound.

When the picture was shown in London, teenagers responded with a wild, uncontrolled fever. They rocked and rioted and tore up the seats in the movie theater.

A year or so after "Rock Around the Clock," Elvis Presley was the top rock-'n'-roll star, not only in America and Britain, but in at least sixteen other countries. Rock was in, and every youngster who could handle any sort of musical instrument, as well as many who couldn't, were imitating Presley and the new rock beat. John, who had gotten a secondhand guitar from Julia, became part of a neighborhood group formed to produce the new beat. "The bloke who thought up the idea," according to John, "didn't get into the group."

Besides John, there were six others, including his friend Pete Shorten playing a washboard. Pete was no musician, but he was a good friend and he wanted to be with his "mate".

The washboard was a homemade instrument favored by skiffle groups springing up in England. A typical skiffle group would have one or two guitars, plus a variety of homemade instruments: washboards for rasping, tea chests for pounding, and various household articles for other sounds.

The boys called themselves the Quarrymen after their school, and they patterned their style on that of Elvis Presley, even copying his long, duck-tailed haircut. They wore their own idea of Teddy-boy clothes, a style reminiscent of Edwardian dress. Elvis and the Teddy-boy clothes are a frightening combination, in retrospect,

Paul McCartney, who attended the same school, joined the Quarrymen a few months after the combo was formed.

As to when the Beatles came into existence, there is some doubt. George Harrison joined the Quarrymen later that year, but John dates the formation of the Beatles from the time he met Paul. "That was the day that it started moving!"

PAUL McCARTNEY'S CHILDHOOD

1942 TO 1956:

Searching for an answer, unsatisfied with his role in life as one quarter of a phenomenon, yet unable to break completely with the Beatle mystique, Paul McCartney remains the baby-faced iconoclast of the group.

He was born James Paul McCartney in Walton Park, a suburb of Liverpool, on June 18, 1942. His father was James McCartney, a forty-year-old center lathe turner in an aircraft factory during the war years. Before the war James had been a cotton salesman.

His mother, Mary Patricia Mohin, a hospital worker, thirty-three when James Paul was born. A Roman Catholic herself, she had the baby baptized, but religion didn't seem to take too well. In fact, as a rule of thumb, it didn't take too well for any of the Beatles. Their ability to ignore most of the civilized facade we live behind makes it difficult for them to swallow any of the cultural mores of our time.

Paul has called himself a "flabby Catholic, and pointed out that if it weren't for the fact that he's, concerned with an afterlife, he'd call himself an atheist. Perhaps it's more of a concern with his image. "But I don't dare come on as an atheist. Look what happened to John when he put Jesus down."

Paul's parents moved back to Liverpool during the war years and Paul's brother Michael was born there in 1944.

Paul was devoted to his brother, according to his father Tim. "They did everything together—especially the things they were told not to. As children, they were inseparable. Wherever one went, the other went too."

The two brothers, according to Jim, were known to their friends as the "Nurk Twins". The name, originating in some childhood joke, was used once by John Lennon and Paul when they were playing guitar together, bored with the uninspired Quarryman label.

Paul, eighteen months older than his brother, was the leader, as Jim remembers it. "He always seemed to know exactly what he wanted, as a baby, and also exactly how to get it. He didn't nag, but he persuaded in the nicest possible way. I guess he was just a born diplomat."

Paul's early boyhood, according to his father, was commonplace, though he searches desperately for some hook to hang a legend on. "He had the fascinating ability to do two things at once."

However, this ability boiled down to watching the "telly" while he did his homework, and not only remembering the program, but doing a good job on the homework as well.

The brothers tumbled through a pleasant childhood while their father tried to get his footing in the confusion of postwar Britain. Paul looks back with sentimentality and love at his mother, who died when he was only fourteen.

Paul started at Stockton Wood Road Primary School and then transferred to Joseph William. "Mother thought the other was becoming too crowded."

Unlike John, Paul was not a bad student, at least according to his father. Paul himself gives a slightly different version of his school days. For one thing, he stresses the fact that he was left-handed. "My mind seems to work in a left-handed way too."

"I seem to do everything from back to front," he once confessed. "I used to write backwards, for one thing. Every time the masters at school looked at my notebooks, they'd throw swinging fits."

School wasn't the only place Paul ran into trouble, according to his own account. "I had a lot of trouble outside of school too. Take a simple thing like riding a bicycle. I never could learn to ride a bike properly when I was a kid because I would insist on pedaling backwards."

The result of course was that he slammed on the brake and fell on his head time and time again, but some mental snag convinced him that his way of pedaling was right and everybody else was pedaling wrong. He just didn't understand why it wouldn't work.

His father finally took Paul out and asked him to explain just what he was doing with the pedals. "Maybe we can find out the trouble," Jim said. "It doesn't seem possible that a boy your age can't ride a bike."

Paul gave his father a demonstration. He hopped on the bike, giving it a little push forward. The momentum carried him on a bit, but as soon as he began to pedal backwards the bike braked to a stop, and tumbled over, pitching Paul into the dust.

His father nodded seriously as he helped Paul up. "I think I have the answer. You're pedaling the wrong way."

Paul flew into a tantrum. "You're just like everybody else," he cried furiously. "That's what they all tell me. I thought you'd be different and help me."

"I'm trying to," Jim McCartney said, fighting to keep a straight face. "That's why I'm telling you that you're riding backwards."

Stubbornly Paul insisted that he was pedaling correctly and everyone else was doing it wrong. Jim thought that one over awhile. "Well, it may be, but then why is everyone else going the right way while you tumble over?"

This reached Paul, who considered the matter for a long time, and at last reluctantly admitted that the world might be right while he was just possibly wrong.

But if he was mixed up about bike riding, he decided, then it was possible that he was also mixed up about his left-handedness. Because his parents and teachers had always urged him to try to change hands, he worked at it and not only found it hopeless, but also built up a massive sense of frustration. According to Paul, that frustration sums up his childhood.

As a young boy he became involved with the Boy Scouts, and Jim encouraged this. He felt that any outdoor life, for a city boy, was bound to be healthy and good. Besides, it included summer camp and a chance to get off the Liverpool streets.

Paul felt that summer camp was the most exciting part of his life. Cooking over an open fire, even if it was only baked beans and sausage, was a totally new experience. In the evening, sitting around the fire, wrapped in blankets, listening to stories and singing songs, he felt completely happy and at peace with his childhood world.

On his return, however, he came down with a severe attack of rheumatic fever and a rash so uncomfortable and stubborn that it wiped all pleasant memories of the summer at camp from his mind.

After primary school, Paul was admitted to Liverpool Institute, a school with a good sprinkling of famous graduates. But in spite of his better academic standing, he gradually began to take the same path that John Lennon had traveled before him. School had no meaning, no clear-cut goal. He didn't know where all the studying was leading him, nor what he would do with it, how he could possibly use it. His father was no example, for he certainly hadn't been able to beat the system. The family only managed to get along because his mother had returned to hospital work and brought in a few pounds.

What then, he asked himself, was the point in his staying on at school? Where would an education lead him?

Class lines were then still pretty clear-cut and it wasn't at all likely that a boy from Paul's class could make any use of an education, in spite of the city's boast that any Liverpool boy who deserved it could get an adequate education.

"So I get it? Then what? Where do I put the thing?"

His discontent with the system was compounded by the working-class neighborhood in which he lived. He was one of the few boys who had gone on to higher education, and his friends resented it and teased him about it.

There were a number of moves for the family after Paul was born, and finally they ended up in Allerton, a suburb of Liverpool. It was a nicer place than any they had lived in before, but unfortunately Paul's mother didn't live to get much pleasure out of it.

At the age of forty-five she died of cancer, a sudden and completely unexpected death for a woman who had devoted so many years of her life to nursing others.

Jim McCartney, at fifty-three, found himself a widower with two lively teenage boys, one twelve and the other fourteen. It was hard, but it could have been worse, according to Jim. They were well-balanced kids. Indeed, to illustrate how well-balanced they were, he tells about an incident that occurred just two years before his wife's death. The two boys were caught stealing apples at a farm near the city. They were with a gang of boys, all about to swarm up the trees and pick the apples, when the farmer appeared. The gang took off, leaving Paul stuck up a tree. Mike ran back to help him, and the farmer caught both and with a show of great indignation, locked them up in his barn, then called their father.

Jim came out and the farmer explained the situation. "Not that they're such bad kids, but maybe you want to teach them a lesson."

Jim did, and in front of the barn he and the farmer put on an act for the boys inside. In raised voices they discussed the possible consequences of the theft. "Do you think they'll get a long sentence? Should we spank them now and not tell the police?"

Finally they opened the bam doors, expecting two well-chastened boys. But instead they got a casual, "Hello Dad. About time you got here."

"I was amazed," Jim said. "But when I talked to them afterwards I discovered that they weren't worried at all since they hadn't actually stolen any apples. And it did make common sense, you know."

It was that kind of common sense, Jim feels, that got the boys through the difficult years immediately after their mother died. It was Jim who seemed most disturbed and torn by his wife's death. He had to be not only father, but mother as well. Fortunately he was a gentle man with a large amount of warmth and decency. It's from Jim, according to Paul, that he inherited or learned whatever charm he has (and that adds up to a considerable amount).

The grief he felt at his mother's death was alleviated to some degree by music and his involvement with the guitar. He was just beginning to learn how to play the guitar about this time.

Jim McCartney had always been musically inclined and back in the twenties had a small band of his own, but his own music, he believes, had no effect on his son. "Very little that I did affected him. In fact, it seemed quite the opposite. I only had to urge something on him for him to drop it. Luckily I kept my mouth shut about music, and that only because I never thought it was that important."

The early rock music moved Paul, but it was Elvis Presley who really started him off. There is no overestimating the impression Presley made on all the young people in Britain at that time. In a very real way he was one of the basic ingredients in the creation of the Liverpool sound. Paul copied Presley—other musical idols ran poor seconds. He began to imitate Presley's hair style as well as his music and he even experimented with the Presley pelvic gyrations.

In 1956 Paul, on an impulse, went along with his friend Ivan Vaughn to hear a neighborhood group play at Woolton Parish Church. The group was called the Quarrymen. It was a casual enough encounter with nothing portentous about it, and yet it was the beginning of the Beatles. Paul went back to hear the group again. He was only fourteen then and they were all older. John Lennon, the .leader, was sixteen, but the two boys hit it off very quickly. There was something both of them had that just locked together. Perhaps it was a crazy kind of attitude toward life, a contemptuous mockery that later became the trademark of the four Beatles, or perhaps it was just a teenage friendship that stuck.

Whatever it was, Paul came back, and eventually was invited to join the Quarrymen. As far as John was concerned, Paul was not only a good guitarist—as good as John himself—but he also resembled their mutual idol, Elvis.

In addition, both boys had lost their mothers at approximately the same age. It formed another bond between them in spite of their age difference.

Paul had already tried his hand at composing, even with no formal knowledge of music, and not to be outdone, John quickly began composing too. Eventually their closeness made it possible for them to compose together, both tunes and words.

At one point the two friends went off hitchhiking to the south to try out in an amateur talent competition. They called themselves the British Everly Brothers, and to their amazement won the top prize. Even the fact that they had to sleep overnight in a roadside ditch on the way back didn't dampen their enthusiasm. They were, they now firmly believed, professionals.

Pete Shorten, about this time, gave in to the growing realization that music was just not his "dish of tea. ... I broke my washboard one night," he recalls, "with an assist from John, who was clowning around. Without a washboard I was nothing, so I just dropped out. I must confess it was with a sigh of relief."

To fill the gap, Paul brought in a friend of his, another boy from his own school who, while he didn't seem to measure up to John and Paul— he was even younger than Paul—still had something the group needed. He also locked in to their way-out sense of humor, though he was far more introverted than the others.

His name was George Harrison. Three of the Beatles had finally gotten together.

GEORGE HARRISON'S CHILDHOOD

1943 TO 1956:

"I never asked to be famous," George Harrison once told a reporter. "I just wanted to be successful."

It would make a good epitaph for a man who has been labeled "the saddest of the Beatles, the one most affected by what he has gained—and lost." To George, probably more than to all the others, the right to personal privacy and individual freedom is most important. The fact that becoming a Beatle has meant an infringement on this right has been saddening and frustrating.

As to living with his own success, George has declared that the only way he can get it out of his system is by becoming a clown as often as he can. "Treat it all too seriously and you go out of your mind."

It's hard to accept statements like these from a boy whose physical identity is so merged in the Beatle image that most adults have trouble picking him out in a group photo. They know he's not Ringo, but which of the other three is he?

"He's the one who never looks straight at you when he's talking," a friend has said in describing him. "He's the one who's always scowling—or thinking."

George—with his apparent ability to see the trap that fame has caught him in—seems the most experimentally inclined of the Beatles, the one constantly looking for new fields to explore. As a child, he probably had the most normal life of any of the four.

He is the youngest of the four, born February 25, 1943. His father, Harold Hargreaves Harrison, was thirty-four years old when George was born. He was a ship's steward during George's early years but later he left the sea and became first a bus conductor and then a bus driver.

His mother, Louise French, was thirty-two when he was born, and just nineteen when she was married. Her first baby, born when she was twenty, was a girl, Louise. Two sons, Harold and Peter, were born six and ten years later. George, born in 1943, had a sister of twelve, and two brothers, seven and three. He was the baby of the family.

George's mother, reminiscing about his childhood, recalls it as a happy one. "George was always full of fun when he was a child. He never caused any serious trouble and even the neighbors liked him a lot, which is unusual with little boys." As if this isn't enough to make her point, she adds, "He loved animals, and I was very proud of the way he liked to help old people."

To underline it again she will dig up anecdotes of baby George giving his money away, or insisting that she give half a crown to an old tramp, "or every old person we met."

George himself remembers those days differently. It seems to him that he was always rebelling and meeting the punishment dealt out to rebels. "Take teachers," he told an interviewer once. "In every class when I was at school there was always a little kid who was too scruffy and smelly. The rest of us were punished by having to sit next to the smelly kid. Fancy a teacher doing that!"

The purity of childhood, George has declared, is quickly lost. "Babies, when they are born, are pure. Gradually they get more impure with all the rubbish pumped into them by society and television and all that—till gradually they're dying off, full of everything."

But unlike the other Beatles, and in spite of his soured attitude toward education, George was a good student. "I don't know why I was," he confessed, "because I didn't actually grind away at the books. I did some studying—one has to—but I wasn't like the boys who boast of spending five hours a day at their work. It just came easy to me. I'd zip through everything. Well, if there was a rea-son it was probably my folks. They kept my nose to the grindstone. I was good at sports too," he recalls. "Made it keen on soccer, cricket, swimming, and all sorts of athletics."

But again and again George insists that he had an uneventful childhood. "Except for my annual illness. Every year, the day before my birthday, I'd develop tonsillitis—up to my thirteenth birthday. The day before I was thirteen I woke up fit as a fiddle. But by then I was used to being sick on my birthday and in spite of the way I felt, I insisted on seeing the family doctor. A good thing too. My throat was fine, but he put me into hospital with nephritis instead!"

According to George's mother, he was destined for greatness at an early age. She saw his development into an entertainer foreshadowed in his childhood. "When he was ten," she says, "his dad gave him some hand puppets. From then on, whenever we had visitors, he always insisted on giving a little show, kneeling behind the couch."

According to his parents, George first began to play the guitar when he was thirteen years old. His interest arose from the fact that his older brother Peter had bought one. George practiced constantly and became quite good at it.

Those were the skiffle group days, and it wasn't hard to get a foursome together with one boy playing a washboard, another a tea chest, and a third a brass pot, especially when the fourth member was as conscientious a guitarist as George.

With a group of his friends, he went to an audition at the Speke British Legion Hall. When the main act failed to turn up, George and his ramshackle group played instead.

They only knew two songs, and when they had finished the second they started the first again, then kept repeating, on and on. Amazingly enough, perhaps on the theory that familiarity breeds acceptance, the audience stayed with them, and at the end of the evening they were given the regular entertainer's fee.

"I remember that night," his mother says. "When they walked into our house afterwards, the fingers of the boy who'd played the brass pot were actually bleeding, he'd played so hard."

But a little blood couldn't dampen the boys' excitement. In their opinion they were no longer playing games. They had performed at a real dance and had received a real fee. They were performers— professionals—and no matter what came up after that, George in his own mind knew that he was a musician.

Fortunately his mother approved of this infatuation with music, and she encouraged his practicing and per-forming. His father had once been a performer of sorts and now he gave his unqualified approval to the boy. "To his music, but not to his clothes," Harold Harrison is quick to say. "George was a wild dresser. Once he decided to do something about his trousers because he didn't want to be old-fashioned. I had bought him a new set of flannels for school, and one day he sat up till late at night altering them on his mother's sewing machine until they were narrow enough for his satisfaction—if not ours."

As a boy, George was taken with cycling. In spite of the fact that during the postwar years, when things were very hard and Harold Harrison had spent some time on the dole, he did manage to buy a bicycle for his son. The new vistas opened up by the mobility of the bicycle fascinated the boy.

"I never knew where he used to get to," his father told a reporter once, "but I suppose he traveled all over the place, not only by bike, but hitchhiking as well."

He recalls one day when George turned up with Paul McCartney and announced that they were going to hitch-hike to the south of England. That night they packed their bags, and the next day they disappeared. He didn't see them again for three weeks, but all the time they were gone they kept sending postcards from places like Southampton and Torquay.

George and Paul went to Liverpool Institute together, George starting in 1954, when he was eleven years old. Before that he had attended the same school as John Lennon, Dovedale Primary, but since there were almost four years between them, John had never noticed George.

By the time George was fifteen, he had become thoroughly hooked on the guitar. Lonnie Donegan was the idol of all the Liverpool teenagers in those days. He had "made it big" as a skiffler who started the British beat with "Rock Island Line". George, like many other music-struck British kids, took Lonnie Donegan as his hero. In 1958, when he was only fifteen, Donegan appeared at the largest theater in Liverpool, the Empire. George begged the money for admission from his parents. He was stunned by the performance, but, not content with going home and sleeping it off or working it out with his guitar, he found out that Donegan was staying with friends in Speke, and he went to the door and hammered on it till Donegan came out. Whereupon George boldly demanded his autograph. Somewhat surprised, the skiffle star agreed and signed for him.

According to George, this experience gave him a deep understanding of the emotional involvement kids go through when they hound the Beatles for autographs. "I never refuse if I can possibly give it to them," he insists.

It was a year later that George bought his first electric guitar. His brother Harold told the story to an interviewer. "Dad wasn't keen on his buying it on hire-purchase. Dad always insisted you shouldn't buy anything unless you had enough money to pay for it."

George, who was an apprentice electrician at the time, working for Blacks, a Liverpool firm, came around to his brother's flat. According to Harold, he went into a long speech about what the group was doing and how much better an electric guitar would be in their act. Realizing what he was working up to, Harold simply sat there, nodding his head and listening.

Finally the punch Sine came out. His dad wouldn't let him have anything on hire-purchase—wouldn't brother Harold sign the guarantee form?

Harold wasn't keen on the idea, but after a great deal of persuasion he agreed and went with George to Hessy's, the Liverpool shop where all the groups bought their instruments.

The guitar George wanted was priced at £120 (approximately $340), quite a sum for his brother to guarantee. To convince Harold, George took it up and began to play it like an expert, but unfortunately no sound came out.

While the embarrassed "pro" struggled with the instrument, a helpful salesman pushed the "on" button and a blast of sound rocked the shop and sent all the instruments on the opposite wall clattering to the floor.

"After that, we were both so embarrassed that I just had to let him get the guitar," Harold said.

The guitar was his, but practicing was another problem. His own home, with the rest of the family constantly present, was hardly conducive. He was finally given the use of a friend's cellar, and this became his rehearsal room. After a while his lonely practicing began to seem meaningless, and he started to invite his friends to "come and use my rehearsal hall."

According to a neighbor, one of the groups that took advantage of this generous offer to share George's cellar was the Quarrymen, with John Lennon and Paul McCartney. A friend of that time says that even then everyone thought that George was something special as a guitarist.

"He was one of the very few people in Liverpool who could play 'Guitar Boogie Shuffle' all the way through." This, according to the neighbors, was the reason he was finally asked to join the Quarrymen.

JOHN, PAUL, GEORGE AND PETE: LEARNING THE TRADE

1956 TO 1959:

The Beatles were in action, not under the name of Beatles, but as three cogs in the musical wheel known as the Quarrymen, three cogs that meshed and turned smoothly. In those days Liverpool was filled with music cellars, the Liverpudlian equivalent of Greenwich Village coffee houses. Low rent and acoustical privacy dictated cellars as the obvious place for small musical groups to make loud musical noises.

For two years, from 1956 to 1958, the boys were semi-amateurs. They played wherever they could, whenever a cellar club or a church dance or a school prom gave them a chance. One of the cellar clubs was called the Casbah, and had been started by a Mrs. Best, a woman whose son was a teenage musician. Mrs. Best said that she started the private club in her own cellar so that she could keep an eye on her boy Peter. She also hoped to give some encouragement to the local teenage combos that were springing up all over Liverpool.

The first time the Quarrymen played at the Casbah was in the summer of 1958. They were brought there by Ken Brown, a friend of Mrs. Best. Ken was a Liverpool boy whose life revolved about the new rock music and his ten-watt amplifier.

Brown, George Harrison, and two other boys, Skinner and Stewart, were playing around on a semiprofessional level as a group called the Les Stewart Quartet. They spent most of their time practicing, however, at the Lowlands Club in Heyman's Green, a section of Liver-pool. Whenever these budding musicians got the chance they would play at any club available, for pay or practice.

Groups of this size had sprouted like mushrooms in all the dark, moist music cellars of Liverpool, but few lasted for any length of time. The Les Stewart Quartet was no exception. Mrs. Best had promised them that they could play at the Casbah, but before the date of their first appearance came around the group had started to fall apart.

Skinner missed the opening date, and an argument between Les Steward and Ken Brown led to Stewart's walking out. Brown and Harrison were only half a group, and in desperation Brown asked George if he knew of two other boys who could join them.

"There's two mates I sometimes play with at Speke," George suggested. "John Lennon and Paul McCartney. Maybe they'd go along."

Paul, fifteen, at the time, was still a schoolboy with an acceptable haircut. But John, at eighteen, was a reluctant artist and something of a beatnik. His long hair fell over the collar of his loud checked jacket, which he wore over skintight jeans. The offer to play at fifteen bob a night (at that time a few cents more than two dollars) thrilled both Paul and John. They would have been well-satisfied to play for nothing, in fact. Most little groups at that time played for experience alone.

At a loss for a good name for the new group, they decided to keep the Quarrymen. It brought them luck, for they became a tremendous hit at Mrs. Best's cellar club, the Casbah,

Brown was the rhythm guitarist of the group, and John and Paul did most of the vocal numbers, while George plunked away faithfully at his guitar, refusing to look the audience in the face. John's pet solo was "Three Cool Cats", which he would growl into the microphone.

Ken Brown liked Paul and George but he felt that some quality about John Lennon just made him less open than Paul and George. "John was moody and withdrawn, a loner who never talked about his family the way the rest of us did," Ken said. "He was very close to his girlfriend, Cynthia Powell, and he seemed to need her in a way none of the rest of us needed girls. Maybe it was just because we were younger."

They played together at the Casbah for nine months but the only thing this period of gestation gave birth to was the loss of Ken. A bad leg kept him out of the group one night, and since he couldn't play, Mrs. Best had him collect money at the door. The other three boys, Paul, George and John, played, without him, but when Mrs. Best decided to pay Ken for the night even though he hadn't played, the others were upset and angry. Ken, they felt, had put something over on them by collecting his share of the fee without playing.

"We think the fifteen bob should be split among us since you didn't play tonight," they told him.

"That's up to Mrs. Best," Ken insisted stubbornly, and Mrs. Best said she thought it only fair to pay him. Ken's stubbornness about the payment, and the others' resentment of his attitude split the group.

After Ken was out, the three tried stubbornly to make it as a trio. They got along with each other so well that they felt reluctant to take anyone else in. But a trio just wasn't in demand. They set out to search for a fourth member and they found one because of a turn which John's life had taken.

John had been living with his aunt after his mother's death, but as the years went by he found that the path he wanted to follow—music first, with art, school, and everything else as a barely tolerated second—was becoming more and more difficult. When he was nineteen years old he finally decided to leave Mimi's house, though he only had a small allowance to live on.

One evening he made his decision openly. "I'm leaving, Mimi. Everyone else at school lives in flats, and I feel like a baby living here at home."

By now his aunt knew him too well to argue the point. "All right," she agreed, to his surprise. "If that's what you want, you can leave."

"I want it," John insisted stubbornly, and then out of guilt at what he was doing, burst out with, "anyway, I can't stand your food."

This was the unkindest cut of all. Mimi had, like the most devoted mother, been lovingly stuffing her nephew with food. "What will you eat if you live in a flat?' she asked unhappily.

John had a quick answer for that. "Chinese food." Leaving a stunned aunt in the kitchen, he packed his bags and moved out. A close friend of John's at art school, Stu Sutcliff, was sharing a flat in Gambria Terrace in the heart of Liverpool with three other boys, and they welcomed John eagerly as one more to share in the rent.

Mimi didn't hear from him for three weeks, and then he dropped in casually, obviously desperately hungry but too proud to accept the meal Mimi offered. He feared it might compromise his independence.

A week later he was back again, and this time Mimi felt that he actually looked thinner. "He sat in the dining room," Mimi remembers, "while I cooked steak and mushrooms, and finally, when he could stand it no longer, he let out a desperate bellow: 'I'm hungry! I'm starving!' "

Mimi fed him happily, and when he complained that he was completely broke, having spent all his allowance on Chinese food, she scraped together another allowance.

However, in spite of his cavalier attitude about money, the living arrangements in the flat seemed to work out, which was more than could be said for his work at art school.

Stu Sutcliff was doing well at school, well enough to win some awards and sell some of his paintings. He became the only boy with available cash.

Nobody knows whether it was the cash, or the fact that Sutcliff was the only one who could be talked into buying a bass guitar, or just that Sutcliff fit in well with the three of them, but eventually Stuart joined John, Paul and George in Ken Brown's place. Now they had a group of four going again.

About this time, one of Sutcliff's paintings was chosen for an exhibition at Liverpool's Walker Art Gallery. John, in spite of his stubbornly slow progress at school, had the ability to appreciate art, and he dragged a reluctant Mimi to see the exhibit and, of course, Stu's painting.

"What do you think of it?" he asked her enthusiastically.

"Well—" There was a long pause, and finally she murmured, "What is it?"

John, in a temper, dragged her out of the gallery, and Mimi, recalling the incident, says, "It really was a shame because I do love art. The picture was just so large I couldn't make head or tail of it."

Perhaps this incident triggered the realization that art was far more complicated than she had imagined, and broke down her last resistance to John's music. At any rate, after that she rarely troubled him about his flagging interest in school. She seemed to settle down to accepting the fact that if the world was losing a Rembrandt, perhaps it was gaining a Beethoven.

While John was attending art school and gradually trampling down his chances of a career in that field, George Harrison was finishing high school, convinced that his own chances in the labor market were growing dimmer and dimmer. He had ended school marked as a poor scholar, and went on to become a shade-less-miserable electrician's apprentice.

What was ahead, he realized, was as bleak a prospect as his father's. He had a working-class background and a working-class future—dull, deadly, and riding the thin edge of poverty and the dole.

Paul too had finished high school and faced the same bleak, empty future. The only area in which any of his group had found acceptance was music. They were sure they had some talent because of their experience in Manchester. John, Paul, George, and Stu had traveled there as a group to try out for the Carroll Levis show, a British television talent-hunt sort of thing. They called themselves

Johnny and the Moondogs because the Quarrymen name was wearing a bit thin by then. They played well and the audience loved them, but unfortunately they couldn't wait for the applause-meter ratings. They had to make the last train back to Liverpool because there wasn't enough money to stay over. As a result, in spite of their audience acceptance, they never qualified for the final judging.

Another example, they felt, of the way poverty could cripple them.

The Moondog name was just one of many they fooled around with in 1958 and 1959. The names of most of the groups featured the leader followed by a group name, such as Rory Storme and the Hurricanes or Barry Starr and the

Co-eds, and since John was the oldest, they had decided on Johnny and the Moondogs. It lasted one engagement.

With Stu Sutcliff on the bass guitar, the boys still felt that they needed a drummer. They had tried to talk Stu into buying drums with his painting money, but he had chosen a guitar because the drums seemed too complicated Since he couldn't play either drums or guitar he felt he should start with the least difficult.

It was in 1959, when the four were struggling to weld themselves into a cohesive whole that they first took on the name of Beatles. There was a group called Buddy Holley and the Crickets and this probably set them thinking along insect lines. With Lennon's facile wit, it wasn't long before he came up with Beatles, punning on the double meaning of "beat": the musical sense, and the beatnik sense. The whole Kerouac-influenced beat movement, though vague and far away, had made some impression on Liverpool, and it appealed to the boys.

Their first big break came when Alan Williams, later owner of the Blue Angel Club, a stronghold for Liverpool's young beat musicians, became their manager. Williams began to book them in all the Merseyside beat shows as the Silver Beatles, the silver being an extra bit of gilding because the boys still didn't feel completely secure with a one-word name.

They auditioned, through Williams, for Larry Pames at the Blue Angel, and they secured their first tour, a fortnight in Scotland, backing Johnny Gentle for £15 (about forty dollars) a week each.

Gentle, a handsome young singer who was just beginning to make it, wondered just what on earth Parnes had sent him when the four baby Beatles arrived. "They were wearing jeans and sweaters and looked like four of the roughest little 'Teds' I had seen in my life," he said.

John and Stu told Gentle that they were in art school and he could well believe it. Their hair fell over their collars and Sutcliff sported a Bohemian beard. George, who was serving his electrician's apprenticeship, looked trim and neat of necessity, and probably because of this became Gentle's favorite. Paul, who was just out of high school, also had a more or less acceptable look.

"This is our big break," John told Gentle breathlessly when they were introduced. "We've been waiting for this."

Gentle's only answer was, "Jesus Christ!"

Though their headquarters on the tour was Inverness, the group was booked into a different dance hall in Scotland every night. To nobody's surprise, the Beatles just couldn't seem to catch on with the girls. They weren't attractive enough for the Scottish lassies. In fact, some of the girls at the dance halls complained to the promoter that the group was no good, and at the end of the first week he decided that the wisest thing would be to let them go and use a local group instead.

John was brokenhearted. He saw their big chance vanishing and all the work they had put into' it going down the drain. He and Stu had taken off from art school with no excuse while Paul and George had lied about vague vacations to get the time off. To see it all come to nothing was more than he could bear. He pleaded with Gentle to intercede. "You know, we thought this was going to be our real big break."

"Yes. You made that pretty clear," Gentle said dryly.

Shrugging despondently, John asked, "Do you blame us?"

Evidently Gentle didn't, and he did feel sorry for them and backed this up with help. He worked out with them in the hotel bar in Inverness, trying out all his numbers over and over again till they were giving him just the right sound.

And it did the trick, because that night, after they had finished their show, for the first time a girl came up to the boys and shyly asked for their autographs. They were all stunned, and delighted. They knew the game well enough to realize that this was the beginning. In music, the beat, the player's skill, the songs, and the technique are all important, but what really makes or breaks a band are the fans, and now they had one!

They came back to Liverpool, delighted with themselves and the tour. No one could fault them now. They were real pros. They had done time on the road and had been paid for it.

HAMBURG AND THE MAKING OF A GROUP

1959 TO 1961

But back in Liverpool the "pros" found that it was as hard as ever to get a real playing date. Tours were one thine their own home ground was another

They drifted back to the Casbah, where Ken Brown their ousted fourth, was now involved with another group the Blackjacks. Mrs. Best's son Pete was the Blackjack's drummer and he had a very impressive, expensive set of drums The Beatles began playing a few dates at the Casbah, and then their next big break came. Alan Williams was auditioning groups for Germany, to play in Hamburg, and he suggested the Beatles.

"But it can't be an all-guitar group," he warned them.

You'll have to get yourself a drummer."

The boys remembered Pete Best then and took off for the Casbah. Ken Brown recalls that afternoon very well tor it was the second time he lost a job because of the Beatles.

"I was sitting in the kitchen with Mrs. Best and Pete having a cup of tea, when the boys tumbled in, all excited. They asked to have a word with Pete and he went outside with them. Then his mother joined them. I wasn't too bothered. After all, Pete and I had built up a good group by then, and I thought our chances were just as good as theirs But Mrs. Best came back to tell me that John, Paul and George had asked Pete to go to Hamburg with them as their drummer."

Ken didn't like it, for after all, it meant the end of the Blackjacks. He was pretty upset, but Mrs. Best, who could be very persuasive, and who was evidently very understanding of the teenage mind, pointed out that they had been offered the season at the Indra, a Hamburg nightclub, and it was just too good an opportunity for Pete I to miss. She knew Ken wouldn't stand in his way, nor want to spoil his future, no sir, not Ken.

"No matter how angry I felt, I had to agree," Ken said.

Pete Best remembers this incident differently. "The boys rang me up and said, 'Do you want to come to Germany? Right! Get your things packed tomorrow.'

The Beatles can't quite remember what happened, except that Pete came with them. The next day the boys, with Stu Sutcliff on the bass

41

guitar and Pete Best on the drums, left for Hamburg by boat. There were some difficulties with parents, but not too many. George was very much on his own because he was considered a working man, and Paul had become quite adept at handling his father. John, of course, had only his aunt to deal with, and since he was living away from home, she presented no problem.

It was during this season in Hamburg that the boys finally decided on a uniform and an image, and a somewhat frightening image it was. Their hair was not unusually long in front, in fact Pete Best seems to have worn a modified crew cut if the pictures taken at the time are to be believed, but their hair curled down on the napes of their necks, and their sideburns were long, a la Presley.

They wore black T-shirts, black leather pants or skintight jeans, and black leather motorcycle jackets.

Paul and George, still not completely across that magic line that divides man from boy, had sullen, angel-baby faces, while John still had the sweet look of childhood.

Pete Best, handsomest in the traditional sense, looked like a nice boy gone wrong and oddly enough, only Stu Sutcliff had a sullen, angry, cadaverous look to his face, odd because Sutcliff was probably the gentlest of the five, never quite up to the teasing and joking of the others.

The Indra, in Hamburg, was located on the Reeper-bahn, a street comparable to the Soho district in London and the Times Square section of New York, an ugly, garish, neon jungle of rock music, called the wildest street in the world and the most sinful.

There was a ten o'clock police curfew for all boys and girls under eighteen, but aside from this there seemed no limits to attendance at the nightclubs. The only strict regulation was against underage children drinking, and eventually the police closed down the Indra for serving minors. By that time the Beatles had worked up a reputation and were able to take the closing in their stride and switch over to the Kaiserkeller down the street.

Hamburg, larger than Liverpool, and wetter, was also far wickeder. Its postwar reputation for sex and sin had spread all over Europe, and its night life was inseparably linked to crime and gangsters.

The Indra, German for India, was a tiny place, but a wild one, and the boys worked hard, learning as they went along. The Kaiserkeller was much larger and they weren't the only Liverpool group booked there. Rory Storme and the Hurricanes were also playing at the Kaiserkeller. The drummer with Storme's group was a bearded boy named Richard Starkey. He had a curly shock of hair that fell forward in a Presley cut, and he affected much more formal clothes than the Beatles—a suit and string tie and a pencil-thin mustache to complement his beard and he drummed with a vague, slightly wild air. But he was good, indeed much better than Pete Best. He played under the name of Ringo Starr.

John, Paul, and George took to him, but there wasn't much time to pursue any friendship. They were kept incredibly busy grinding out show after show.

It was a hard, grueling engagement in the smoke and stink of the cellar nightclub, sleeping in miserable quarters, eating irregularly and improperly, and working eight hours a day for the equivalent of forty American dollars a week for each of them. They lived in a couple of rooms over a cinema, Peter, Paul, and a singer, Tony Sheridan, sharing one room; John, George, and Stu sharing the other. Sheridan, who became one of Germany's top pop singers, says those days were grim. "Just that one attic with no windows and only a fanlight in the roof. When it rained, we were soaked. No carpets, no heating, no running water. Just a basin and stand and a jug for washing."

They slept in six army bunks in the two rooms and ate nothing but cornflakes. "The place got filthier and filthier," Sheridan says. "We slept in the same bedclothes for a month or so at a time because we couldn't afford to have them cleaned."

Arid yet the season was probably the making of the Beatles as a group. It was a fire that welded them into tough professionals.

At least this was true for four of the five. Stu Sutcliff, less a musician and still more an artist, met a German girl, Astrid Kichener, an artist and photographer, and her friends. Gradually these friends, students, began coming to hear the boys play. They were an intellectual group, mostly art and philosophy students, and to the boys from Liverpool they presented a new and fascinating insight into a different world.

Astrid was an excellent photographer, and she saw something exciting and photogenic in. the boys' physical appearance, the kind of vitality, she said, that James Dean had. They were representative, to her and her German intellectual friends, of the new youth, the new rebellion.

Most likely she saw in them some of the magic that was later to capture the wild devotion of the youth of Europe and America. She took many photographs of the boys, employing skill and imagination to bring out the qualities she found.

These pictures are among the best ever taken of the Beatles, at least in capturing the elusive sexual attractiveness that the boys were developing.

While all the Beatles liked Astrid, a deeper romance quickly developed between Stu Sutcliff and the girl. They were engaged in a few months, and when the season was over and the other Beatles went back to Liverpool, Stu stayed behind with Astrid for a while to make plans for the future.

The end of the Hamburg stay was less than triumphant. They had arranged with the manager of Hamburg's Top Ten nightclub, a place far superior to the Kaiserkeller, to appear there, but just as the contract was signed, the authorities discovered that George was only seventeen 'years old and thus underage.

He was promptly deported, and the others played only one night at the Top Ten before a minor brush with the police landed them in trouble. In the end they all went back to England.

That was December of 1960, and to the five of them it seemed as if the Beatles, as a group, were finished just a bare few months after they had started.

The boys had come home one by one, exhausted by the long engagement, discouraged and tired. But after a few weeks their natural youthful bounce took over and they began getting together again for rehearsals.

Their style had set during their Hamburg days into a compelling, wild, rhythmic technique with a strong driving beat. Bob Wooley, a disk jockey from Liverpool, reported in a local beat-scene paper that they had resurrected rock 'n' roll after it had been emasculated by men like Cliff Richards. Their music is "the stuff screams are made of," he said, adding that it was "musically authoritative, physically magnetic." He spoke of the "mean, moody magnificence of Pete Best, a sort of teenage Jeff Chandler."

On their return from Germany they played first at the Casbah, their old training ground, and still managed by Pete Best's mother. Rory

Storme, back from Hamburg too, was also at the Casbah, and they renewed acquaintance with his wild drummer, Ringo Starr.

While both the groups had been in Hamburg, the Casbah had become an active night spot in Liverpool. When the boys opened there, a friend, Neil Aspinall, who was training to be a chartered accountant, drew enormous posters reading, "RETURN OF THE BEATLES, DIRECT FROM HAMBURG!"

Brian Kelly, a promoter, came to see them and liked what he saw. He began to find them modest bookings at Litherland Town Hall and Aintree Institute.

It was in the autumn of 1961, short of a year after their return from Hamburg, that the boys began to play at the Cavern, the music cellar that was their first springboard to fame.

Sam Leach, a music promoter, described one of the early appearances of the Beatles in the Cavern: "Four young, quiet-looking boys preparing their equipment prior to' the performance; teenage girls excitedly crowding around the stage, hoping to catch the eye of their particular Beatle idol. The proverbial calm before the storm.

Then a breathless count, and the four, black-leather jacketed young men crash into their first high-powered number. A tousle-haired jack-in-the-box call Paul McCartney leads the fantastic, pulsating, soul-shattering vocal with every ounce of energy he possesses."

This was the point in 1961 at which they burst upon a music-happy Liverpool. At Litherland Town Hall, during their first engagement, Paul suddenly launched into their Hamburg success, the song "Long Tall Sally," and the audience stormed the stage. None of the audience had ever seen anything like the boys, according to Neil Aspinall, who helped them set up their equipment. It was as if they had happened overnight.

Pete, the drummer, was also the comedy man, and during those days could bring the house down in wild laughter over his singing of "Matchbox." George, too, sang comedy numbers, and John and Paul did the specialties, such as

"We're Gonna Dance in the Street Tonight," and "Tutti Frutti." Stu Sutcliff, still more of an artist man than a musician, was unbelievably shy on stage. When he had to sing, he I would resort to tender love ballads, usually with his back to the audience. Success now seemed to key all five of them up to an unbearable pitch. They were nervous performers, terribly self-conscious about their tender years and a little bewildered (even though delighted) by the growing hordes of • screaming fans. To overcome their self-consciousness and nervousness they played the clown. This was particularly true of Paul, who onstage or off was a constant comedian.

But John, too, had a comic touch, and often was grotesquely wild onstage. At one performance, after finishing a number, he took a fantastic leap into the air and split his skintight jeans. A few nights later it happened again, to the delight of the audience, and John took advantage, of the accident, turning it into a regular thing, showing the split to the audience and screaming, "Look! I've done it again."

They rarely sang together as a group during this period, but instead each would take a torn with his own particular solo specialty. It wasn't until a second tour took them back to Hamburg that they matured enough to develop a style of close harmony, a tremendous step forward.

There was evidently something about sinful Hamburg that acted as a force to weld musical styles out of raw talent. Their first visit developed the wild, solid, sexual beat that lifted them to Liverpool's elite, and their second visit developed their close harmony.

On that second visit to Hamburg, George, who was eighteen, was allowed to stay out the tour. Stuart, who had been corresponding regularly with Astrid, finally decided that art, not music, was his strong point, and he regretfully left the group and stayed behind in Hamburg with her.

While in Hamburg the Beatles had cut some records for a German recording company, one of them called "My Bonnie." The records sold poorly and were soon almost forgotten, except by a few early fans.

The boys returned to' Liverpool and the Cavern, and their meteoric rise to fame continued. The Cavern became their home ground, and a growing flood of teenage fans flocked to hear the Beatles, the "Silver" dropped from their name for good.

Their music, while still essentially a variant of rock V roll, began to improve as they developed a style of their own. But the improvement in their music was accompanied by ho improvement in their clothes. They still looked like young hoods with their black leather jackets, tight leather pants, black T-shirts, wild hair, and long sideburns.

But musically they were harmonizing as well as any of the top

American singing groups. The world-famous Mersey sound was being born.

In 1961, five months after their return from Hamburg, they made a debut at the Tower Ballroom in New Brighton, where they attracted a crowd of 40,000, estimated as the largest audience ever drawn by a musical ; rock group in Liverpool.

During this dizzy ascent, the boys were hardly more than teenagers themselves. John was all of twenty in 1960, when they began to catch on; Paul was eighteen and George seventeen. Two years later they were kings of the English musical mountain.

During the days at the Cavern they found time to function as somewhat normal teenagers, though there wasn't any time to develop their education. On this score their parents had finally given up coaxing. The entertainment business, they were beginning to realize, far from being a way to waste time, was a sure bonanza. Their sons had, overnight, changed from "music bums" to musicians.

During this period, when they had to play any distance from Liverpool, they turned to Neil Aspinall for help. His accounting yawned in front of him as a deadly, boring abyss, and any excuse to help these lively, exciting friends was welcome. They had an old blue van, which Neil drove, and from occasional chauffeur he gradually turned into a road manager. Finally the manager of the Cavern offered them a block of fifty evening engagements plus a string of lunch sessions. The money from this enabled them to hire Neil on a full-time basis for a little more than six pounds a week. Neil accepted, and Paul McCartney was the next to decide that maybe music was a full-time occupation. At the time he was working as "second mate" to a truck driver, helping to unload material for a cable firm and making about fifteen pounds a week. Since the truck job didn't involve long-distance hauls that would require him to sleep over on the road; Paul was able to play with the boys in the evenings. But lunch sessions were out, and when the Cavern offer came, the other three pressured him to give up his trucking job. "I can't give it up," he protested. "It's steady and it's fifteen pounds a week. That's good money, you know." "As far as money goes, you'll get almost two pounds each lunchtime," John argued. "That's not fifteen pounds!" "Sod you, then," John shouted angrily. "We'll play without you!" But when the first lunch session came, Paul was there, waiting for the rest. "Thought you were working?" John asked blandly.

"You think too much. Besides, I gave that all up. Never did like hauling cables about—big ruddy things they are!"

While Neil may have regretted his choice in the beginning, wondering what future if any a road manager had, he says that "once the boys took off, there were no regrets. It was all excitement and adventure and things happening. I didn't miss accounting,"

Of course the money improved and eventually became far more than accounting would ever have provided.

The van the boys were carted around in was also used to take their girlfriends out on dates. Two little blond waitresses at the Jacaranda coffee bar on Slater Street in Liverpool, where the boys would sometimes play, remember those days and the van. The coffee bar, they said, was a second home to the Beatles.

Paul, they recall as a "smashing dancer," and the rest as "ever so friendly." They also remember that "nearly every night the boys took us about in their van to all the places they used to play."

The boys went through a succession of girlfriends in those days in rather healthy fashion, all except John, who, if the stories are to be believed, remained faithful to Cynthia Powell. It may well be so, for Cynthia has gone on record as saying, "He has not changed from the first day I met him. I understand everything he does. He may surprise many, but never surprises me."

Those were probably the last years they could ever have a normal relationship with girls. Teenage idolatry makes such a thing almost impossible. Pete Best says that the first time they were mobbed by teenage girls was at Litherland Town Hall on St. Valentine's Day.

They were playing the Elvis Presley tune, "Wooden-Heart," and afterwards they planned to have Paul, as the handsomest, present a real wooden heart to some girl from the audience.

One girl was selected to come on stage, but instead a mob of hundreds surged up. Paul disappeared, screaming, under a wave of nubile nymphs. Far from being alarmed, the boys all thought it was great. "After that it seemed to happen everywhere," Paul recalls wistfully.

BRIAN EPSTEIN BECOMES THE BEATLES' MANAGER

1961 TO 1962

In the fall of 1961, a young boy in jeans and black leather jacket, Liverpool's teenage uniform, came into the North End Music Store, NEMS, and asked for "My Bonnie". NEMS was one of a chain of music departments in the group of furniture stores owned by the Epstein family and managed by Brian Epstein.

"It's a record made in Germany by a new group that call themselves the Beatles," the boy said.

Brian Epstein had never heard of the Beatles, but he prided himself on being able to obtain any record requested, and he promised to try to find it.

Before Epstein had time to check, two young girls came in and asked for the same record.

Only three inquiries in two days, but they made Epstein curious enough to search out the group at the Cavern, a beat music club in a disused warehouse underneath Liverpool's Mathew Street. Epstein described the club as a "spot where jazz was replaced with raw, made-in-Liverpool beat music, usually played on loudly amplified guitars and drums."

In telling of his visit, he has said that, dressed as he was, he was apprehensive at the idea of marching in among a group of rough teenagers, wearing T-shirts, jeans, and motorcycle boots and jackets. It was unthinkable, to Epstein, to discard his elegant clothes, although he realized just how inappropriate they would be in the Cavern.

He wasn't a member of the club but he pulled a few

He quickly grew disenchanted with acting and again returned to his father's business, determined to stick to this profession for a while. He was now twenty-three. Part of the furniture store consisted of a large record section, and it was here that Brian really found himself.

The music departments of the Epstein chain of furniture stores were called NEMS, an acronym for North End Music Stores, and under Brian's dedicated management they flourished. For four years Brian played the part of a serious business executive, intent on building up the NEMS enterprise and proving to himself and the world that he could hold a job for as long as he wanted to and do it well.

However, by 1961 creeping boredom set in, and his interest in the role began to lag. "Life was getting too easy," he said as an excuse, "and I wondered how I could expand my interests."

The answer came with the inquiry after a Beatle record. Brian Epstein was ripe for a new role and a new job, boy manager.

After watching them at the Cavern, Brian had spoken to the four Beatles and suggested that getting together for a meeting might be beneficial to all of them. The boys, impressed by Brian's elegance and "posh" manner in spite of their tendency to joke at such things, were just about ready for some direction. They had been "managed" in a loose sense by one or two men connected with the Cavern, disk jockeys and promoters who would get them bookings in a casual way. Alan Williams had gotten them a few dates around Liverpool, but none of the bookings had seemed to really exploit their talent.

"What we need," John said, "is someone who cares about us, who'll build us up a bit and get us into the big time."

Paul agreed. "We've got something or the kids wouldn't hang around us at the Cavern like they do. What we need is a real manager."

George and Pete agreed, and they decided to meet with Epstein and see what he had to offer. "But we mustn't be too eager," Paul warned the others. "We won't rush into anything."

The first formal meeting between Epstein and the four Beatles, however, was less than auspicious. Only Pete, John, and George arrived on time.

Epstein began to pace the office and then fume in annoyance. He finally called Paul at home and to his amazement was informed that "the boy is taking a bath."

He scowled at the three Beatles who were watching him innocently. "It's disgraceful. He's going to be very late."

"But he'll also be very clean," George pointed out with a straight face.

The meeting, when it finally got going, was not a failure, but then it was not a success either. Success and agreement came after two more meetings, during which time the four boys slowly grew to like this quiet, elegant, and prematurely middle-aged music seller, and Epstein, on his part, felt a "strong irrational attraction to the four."

"Quite simply," he told them at a third meeting, "you need someone to manage you. Would you like me to do it?"

After a long pause, John blurted out, "Yes." The rest agreed, but Paul asked uneasily, "Will it make much difference to us? I mean, it won't change the way we play?"

Epstein assured them that it wouldn't.

A contract was drawn up, and then Epstein set out on the long, discouraging effort to get the group accepted by one of the big record companies. His concept of managing them was a cut above arranging their grueling tours and dates at the Liverpool clubs. He knew that if they were ever to amount to anything they would have to cut a record. That way lay not only popularity but the sweet touch of gold.

An audition with Decca Records was finally promised, and the boys and Brian took off for London full of hope and excitement, but the audition was a disappointment.

The boys' music was taped, and after careful consideration the Decca officials turned them down. "We don't like your boys' sound," they told Brian, and added the friendly advice that, anyway, groups of four were on the way out.

In spite of Decca's disinterest, the boys' faith in themselves grew stronger. When Brian began to wonder if promoting them was worth all the effort he was putting into it, they convinced him that it was just a matter of time before they would be discovered by the music world. In the meantime they felt that they were doing well playing the Liverpool scene for fifteen pounds a night.

Their conviction that they were good was not simply ego. The Cavern was haunted now by a growing army of fans, mostly girls, who screamed eagerly at the sight and sound of the boys and struggled to talk to them, touch them, or even just stare at them.

Once again Brian, armed with the Beatles' tape, attempted to storm the disinterested recording bastions of London. This sally resulted in a meeting with George Martin, an executive at Parlophone, a small arm of the very large Electric and Musical Industries Ltd., or "EMI" the British part of America's Capitol Records.

Martin and Epstein hit it off well, and it suddenly seemed as if there was a chance for producing a Beatle record.

Martin was more than an executive and senior producer for EMI. A lean, precise Londoner, with hair as short as the Beatles' was long, he had a classical musical background that included time as second oboist in the old Sadler's Wells orchestra.

Martin was also a fine electronics man and had been working with Parlophone since 1950. Most of his work had been supervising the production of records featuring sophisticated humorists, such as Flanders and Swann, Peter Sellers, and Peter Ustinov.

But the big recording money lay in singers or groups, and Parlophone simply couldn't come up with any. Martin desperately hoped that he could find one and, through producing a hit, secure his own position at EMI. When Epstein approached him with the Beatle tape he thought that this group might just be the one he needed for a hit. He liked their sound, though he thought it could be improved, and with his knowledge and skill at electronics he might just be the man to improve it.

"I didn't do any double somersaults," he recalls. "The material on the tape wasn't that good, but I liked them well enough to offer them a recording contract, and I started them out with a firm hand. I told them very much what to do."

A recording session was arranged between Epstein and Martin, and Epstein returned to Liverpool and the eager Beatles for a wild celebration over the "breakthrough."

When the four boys finally went up to London to meet Martin, he took to them as readily as he had taken to Brian. Their first meeting ended with Martin telling the boys, "Let me know if there's anything you didn't like."

George Harrison, with a bland face, said, "Well, for a start, I don't like your tie."

It was that kind of flat humor that Martin enjoyed, and it was a good thing for the boys and himself that he did, for over the years George Martin's genius with electronics and his ability to blend and mix sound tracks has added a tremendous amount of depth to the Beatles' music. Without his help they probably wouldn't have the reputation they now have.

John and Paul had been composing music together since they had first teamed up. They would work out the tunes and words in a truly cooperative fashion, batting ideas back and forth until they shaped up into words and music but neither thought much of these mutual creations. At this time their most successful numbers had been written by other composers: "Long Tall Sally" and "My Bonnie."

They were diffident about playing their own tunes, especially at a recording session. "But after all," John told Paul, "if we turn out to amount to something, why not get our own tunes plugged?" So at that first recording session the Beatles did one number that Paul and John had composed together, something called "Love Me, Do."

Martin liked the tune, but he had some reservations about Pete Best's work on the drums, reservations that the other three Beatles were beginning to share. In addition to these musical doubts they felt that Pete just didn't fit in with them in general. He was too "conventional" for the group. He was friendly with John, but neither Paul nor George felt close to him.

In spite of this he accompanied them on a third tour to Hamburg, undertaken while they were waiting for an answer from Parlophone. Despite Martin's enthusiasm, the small affiliate of EMI hadn't yet committed itself to signing them up.

When they went to Hamburg this time they were in a higher income bracket, and they were able to fly over, full of jubilance and excitement. But their bubble of exhilaration was punctured at the airport, where a tearful Astrid met them with the news of Stuart Sutcliff's death from a brain tumor.

Pete Best, describing the incident, said, "Astrid was sobbing. We all felt it was unthinkable; we just couldn't take it in. I think John was hit the hardest. After all he had known Stu the longest and he was closest to him."

They went onstage the following night and managed to' conceal what they felt, but Pete said they kept thinking of Astrid and Stu during the entire performance.

According to Pete Best there had been some ill feeling within the group before Sutcliff left it. John, Paul, and George used to tease Stu about being "square and thick." For that matter they picked on Pete, too, for Pete and Stu were much too easy-going for them. One of the three had even tangled with Stu, once at the entrance to the club and once on stage. "But it was really kid stuff," Pete said. "We all squabbled in those days. But in spite of the squabbling, John felt very close to Stu, like a brother, and Stu's death came as a terrible blow."

How much of the reaction was guilt at the teasing treatment they had accorded Stu is hard to say. When the boys were dissatisfied with a member of the group, they could be very hard on him, Stu's performance was never equal to the others', nor for that matter was Pete's, and he too felt some rough treatment from John, Paul, and George.

Stu's death cast a cloud on the entire Hamburg tour, but a cable from Epstein helped put them back on their feet. Parlophone, with EMI behind it, had signed the boys. The cable read: "EMI contract signed, sealed, tremendous importance to' all of us, wonderful."

Paul sent back a picture postcard of the Reeperbahn, saying, "Please wire 10,000 pounds advance royalties!" John wrote, "When are we going to be millionaires?" and George, manfully plunking away at his guitar, scribbled, "Please order new guitars."

Back in England on September 11, 1962, they made their first Beatle record for Parlophone, "Love Me, Do," and on the flip side, "P.S. I Love You," both Lennon-McCartney compositions.

In only a few days the record was among the top twenty in Great Britain.

Two months later they issued "Please Please Me," also composed and written by Lennon and McCartney. This became a runaway best seller, leading every other record in the country.

Epstein, attempting to push the boys toward a little more publicity, kept running into a noticeable lack of enthusiasm on the part of the British columnists, in spite of the Beatles' popularity with the young set. It took a little while for him to realize that the columnists' distaste sprang not from their opinion of the boys' music, but from their antipathy to the Beatles' appearance. The latent brutality that had made the little girls' hearts pound simply turned the columnists' stomachs.

Epstein promptly "redid" the boys, buying them new suits, black waistcoats and trousers, white shirts, and black silk knitted ties. He also restyled their hair in long, casual, over-the-forehead bangs.

Soon after, John, Paul, and George approached Epstein with, "Now you're our manager and we're not happy with Pete Best's drumming. We've talked to the drummer with Rory Storme and the Hurricanes and he'll come over to us. Richard Starkey, goes by the name of Ringo Starr. We really get along with him, so we want Pete out and Ringo in. You arrange it."

It was a rough chore for Brian Epstein, but he faced up to it manfully and made an appointment with Pete to "talk things over."

"Pete," Epstein said, "arrived on time as quiet as ever. I guess he knew what was coming."

Epstein told him what the boys had decided, and though he tried to offer a few other possible outs for Pete, even that he be the center of a new group which Brian could manage, Pete was crushed and left upset and depressed.

He failed to turn up for an engagement at the River Park Ballroom in Chester, according to Brian, and he never again played with the Beatles.

Neil Aspinall, who had been a close friend of Mrs. Best and Pete before he met the other three Beatles, felt torn by the firing of Pete, but he finally decided to stick with John, Paul, and George. He became their road manager in earnest, accepting a formal salary from Brian Epstein, and gave up all pretense of accounting. He remained one of their two road managers for years, as long as they toured. The other road manager was Malcolm Stevens, a husky young man from the Cavern Club.

Pete's firing wasn't taken lightly by the Beatle fans, and for a while it looked as if there would be mass riots at the concerts given by the new Beatles with Ringo on the drums. Fans demonstrated and carried placards saying, "Pete yes, Ringo no!" "Pete forever, Ringo never!"

Ringo, however, was a success with the Beatles themselves from the start. He shaved his beard and mustache, washed the grease out of his hair, combed it forward, and became "pure Beatle."

Eventually the excitement died down and even Rory Storme, who took Ringo's loss ungraciously, relented and wished them all luck. The final set of four Beatles was launched, if not in a wild balloon, then possibly in a yellow submarine.

RINGO STARR'S CHILDHOOD

1940 TO 1962

"I still can't get over the way I've been accepted as a Beatle. A drummer expects to take a back seat. I couldn't see any reason why the fans would want me to do anything but drum. I'm still knocked out by the whole thing." This was Ringo, four years after he had joined the group.

The Quiet Beatle, the Domesticated Beatle, the Miserable Beatle, and the Sad Beatle—Ringo has been labeled all of these, but the question still remains. Which is he?

According to his Beatle companions, he's none of these. He's the one who can, without effort, drop a perfect punch line into any dressing-room conversation. In fact, he's the Beatle who coined the phrase, "a hard day's night."

"The thing is," he's often said, "I've got one of those faces that doesn't smile very much. I'm feeling good inside, having a great time, but it just never shows."

Onstage, Ringo sits apart from the other three, and he rarely sings. In answer to this, Ringo said, "Sitting apart's a whale of a lot better than wearing a carnation in your buttonhole so people can tell who you are. It ain't likely anyone else around will be wearing a set of drums!"

Possibly Ringo is the bluntest, and most certainly he's the most proletarian of the Beatles. "But I'm not thick," he's defended himself, "I'm just uneducated."

It's apparently true, for he seems less complicated but a good deal more mature than the others. Of all four, he gives the impression of being the most content—satisfied with life, and grateful for what he has.

His courtship of Maureen Cox, now his wife, is typical of his approach to life—slow, gentle, and direct. He met her at the Cavern only five days after he had joined the Beatles. She was only fifteen, a dedicated Beatle fan who nevertheless felt sorry for the new drummer who was taking more of a drubbing than his own drums from the angry pro-Best faction. Because of this sympathy, she put herself out to be particularly nice to him, and he finally responded one evening.

"Take you home, girl?" he offered.

She came right back with a snappy, "Okay." Then quickly added, for these Beatles had built up a reputation in more than music, "But I have my girlfriend with me."

Ringo had no driver's license, but he had a car. He took both the girls home after the show, not only that night, but every night for the next two months. "The three of us was getting very friendly," he said.

One day he moved in for the kill. "Could we go out one night? Could it be just you and me?"

Maureen, with a gift for lean dialogue, said, "Okay."

It took two years for them to get married, but Ringo said, "Ah well, I was always the marrying type. Anyway, I was rich already so it didn't matter."

According to the record, Ringo was born Richard Starkey on July 7, 1940, in Liverpool. Three days after his birth the Battle of Britain began and the Luftwaffe launched the first of the devastating saturation bombings of England; Liverpool taking a beating second only to that given London.

Although no junior was appended to his name, he was the son of Richard Henry Parkin Starkey, who was in the candy business. Elsie Gleave, his mother, was twenty-six when he was born and Richard Senior was a few years older, but no one—even Ringo—seems to know exactly how old.

Ringo was born on Madryn Street in Liverpool in the dock area called the "Dingle," historically one of the toughest areas of Liverpool. Ringo, however, has refused to acknowledge that it is, or ever was, a slum.

"I loved it round there," he said once. "Our neighbors have been great to me, and since I found fame and fortune they've kept an eye on Mum and Dad whenever I've been away."

Ringo was an only child, and his parents were divorced before he was old enough to remember his father. Most of his childhood memories seem to center about illnesses. "When I was six and a half I had appendicitis. I remember being carried downstairs to the ambulance. I saw all my aunties and uncles sitting around the kitchen as I passed. At the hospital, the doctor kept bashing me in the stomach—or so I thought. I remember thinking he shouldn't do that. I wasn't well!"

The appendicitis developed into peritonitis, and he spent six months in the hospital. When he was ready to be discharged, a fall from his bed put him back in the hospital for another six months.

This missed year set him back physically and academically. "I don't think I ever made up the schooling I missed."

At Dingle Vale Secondary Modem school this was not surprising. The only thing that stands out clearly in Ringo's mind from those days is what happened to the lunch money his mother gave him each day. "She always gave me enough to buy a decent lunch, but it seemed to me that it was a pity to waste all that money on food. I'd buy four-penny-worth of chips and a chunk of bread and save the rest of the money for visits to the flicks."

The family skidded along on the thin edge of poverty, his mother working as a barmaid, then a fruit seller, but always working. In spite of this, Ringo maintains that they had a nice home. "We didn't ever live in squalor."

Squalor, of course, exists mainly in the eyes of the beholder. Ringo beheld that early world with steady eyes. His mother, he insists, gave him the best she could. If he wanted something beyond her means, she'd say, "I'll try and get it," rather than letting him down with a flat, "No." "When she did promise something, she never failed me," he recalls fondly.

The boy was given a great deal of freedom, possibly because his mother's work made it impossible for her to police him. The extra freedom didn't hurt him, but his health remained fragile, and at fourteen, a bad cold put him back in the hospital for a year. When he came out after this stint, he found himself hopelessly behind in his schoolwork.

His mother had remarried when he was thirteen years old, but he still wonders at the fact that she asked his permission before the wedding. "I loved Harry Graves, my new father, anyway," he said. "He'd been coming around for four or five years and was already like a dad to me. But it was nice to know I counted enough to be asked."

Of his stepfather, he also says, "Harry is a gentle man, a gentleman too. He loves kids and animals, and they love him."

Harry rounded out Ringo's life. He was every bit of a real father to the boy, though with none of the emotional tugging and pulling of a real father. He evidently encouraged Ringo's preoccupation with music, and when the boy got out of the hospital after his second stint, his step- father bought him a set of drums.

School by now was a hopeless muddle. Ringo knew he had missed far too much ever to catch up, even if he wanted to, and he also knew he didn't want to. So with a sigh of relief he left the school for good and started looking around for a job.

He had no trade at this point, and he didn't do well at unskilled jobs. For one thing he was physically small and not very strong. He lasted a week as a railroad messenger, and two awful weeks in the merchant navy.

Harry introduced him to a friend who knew another friend who was a wood joiner. Young Richard was apprenticed to the joiner and worked for six months as an apprentice, but saw no signs of a regular job in the field. There were just no vacancies among joiners, so he switched to engineering at the suggestion of his boss and became an apprentice engineer.

The drums were his true love during this time, and the deeper he became involved with the world of labor, the more time he spent practicing the drums.

Finally he heard about an opening for a "skin" man with a group called the Darktown Skifflers, and he applied for an audition.

He remembers that he competed against nearly a dozen other drummers, all, he was sure, better than he was. He left the audition in despair, sure that he was the worst of the lot, but to his amazement the leader of the group came to his house the next day and told him he had the job.

For a while he kept up his apprenticeship and played with the Darktown Skifflers, but then an offer came along to play for the summer at Butlins, a holiday camp in North Wales. He was to play with a group led by an old friend of his, Alan Caldwell, who, under the name of Rory Storme, headed the Hurricanes.

The pay was the equivalent of forty-five dollars a week, and when he heard that, he knew where his future lay and it wasn't in engineering. He gave up his apprenticeship, much to his family's disgust. "You'll be back in three months," his boss predicted, and his mother urged him to stay an apprentice at least another year. "You'll have a trade," she argued. "Who knows? Even if you get to be successful at music, how long can this music craze last?"

The summer, away from dirty Liverpool, was a wonderful experience for Ringo. He recalls it as "all fun except for one unhappy incident."

Rory, who' was a qualified swimming instructor, persuaded Ringo, who had never learned to swim, to plunge into the lake and try. Ringo agreed and did so well that Rory decided to teach him underwater swimming too. Somehow the two became separated, and Ringo panicked and began to shout and flail the water.

Rory reach Ringo just as he was going under for the third time and dragged him out. At that point, Ringo says, he knew once and always that he was "a city boy."

Remembering that summer, Ringo claims it developed whatever talent he has for adlibbing on stage and managing an audience. "It was the best experience I could have had. Those audiences at the holiday camps were tough ones. If a performer could hold his own with them I say he could do well anywhere.

"They used to heckle us something fierce, and that taught me a lot of things. Mainly it taught me good stage sense, knowing when to come back at the audience with flip answers, and when to keep quiet and ignore the whole flap.

"Any tune we asked for requests from the audience, like as not they would name tunes none of us had ever heard of or played before. We learned to adlib musically, faking the tune if someone would sing a few bars to cue us.

"Eventually we got so we could play anything to order, as often as not with no sort of musical arrangement at all."

This was all the more surprising in view of Ringo's total ignorance of written music. "I can't read drum music even now," he admits. "I wish I could. I know I'd be a much better drummer if I could, but I have a good ear and a good memory. I may not always play a number the same way twice in a row, but I keep the beat and see that we always finish together."

For the record, it should be observed that Ringo has been proclaimed by some men who are in a position to pronounce judgment as "the best damn man in his field."

The fact that he was playing in a professional band meant more to the boy than simply a steady income, though that too was no mean thing. In fact he has claimed that his involvement with music was a strong factor in keeping him out of delinquency.

"When I was sixteen, you know," he once said, "I used to walk on the road with the rest of the lot and we'd have all our drape coats on and we'd have a few laughs with the rival gangs, and then I got the drums and the bloke next door and I got a job and we started playing together and another bloke and me made a bass out of an old tea chest and this was about 1958, mind you, and we played together and then we started playing on dances and things, you know, and we took an interest in it and we stopped going out and hanging around comers every night."

Rory's mother, Vi Caldwell, remembers Ringo as her favorite of all the boys she came in contact with in those days, "and there were quite a few, with Rory dragging them all home." Ringo, she recalls, "had such marvelous eyes, so full of feeling, so sympathetic."

Sympathetic or not, Ringo got on well with Rory and his band. After the summer holiday camp they played the American military bases. They also did the "Hamburg bit" where Ringo met the Beatles. Acquaintanceship ripened into friendship and the decision to join the Beatles when he was asked.

It is interesting that Ringo's version of how he came to replace Pete Best in 1962 is quite different from Pete Best's version. According to Ringo, he was playing with the Hurricanes when Pete Best became ill. Ringo was to fill in for one show. Although they weren't famous yet, the Beatles were earning the biggest money in. Liverpool. Ringo recalls that he was offered five pounds for that one date.

"The drummer went sick again," he said, "and I played with them again. I played, oh, eight or nine times like that, filling in a day at a time."

According to this version, when it seemed obvious that Pete Best wouldn't be able to return, the Beatles asked Ringo to join the group on a permanent basis.

Before Ringo joined the Beatles, he had been experimenting with different haircuts. "I used to change it every couple of months," he said. "Up, down, sideways—anything to get a little attention up there on stage."

The Beatles told him, "Get your hair flattened down, and shave off the beard, but you can keep your sidies."

"I kept them. We didn't originate these cuts, you know. It's been done this way for thousands of years."

It's a reflection on Ringo's good nature that even after he had split with Rory Storme he remained on close terms with Rory's mother. More than that, for if her memory is correct, he brought the other three Beatles around to her from time to time for a little mothering.

Mrs. Caldwell remembers that many a night, after a late date, the boys would drop in for a visit, "flopping into chairs and drinking cup after cup of tea and chatting until the early hours of the dawn."

"Ringo was very quiet in those days," Mrs. Caldwell said. "He could be depressing. Just sitting in a chair not saying a word all evening, or staring with those sad eyes of his." However, she is quick to deny that his silence may have been simply a lack of anything to say, or that his lack of animation was simple content. It is always more interesting to' evoke the image of a silent, brooding introvert. The truth is, as Ringo insists, that he just wasn't up to the others' level of wit and vitality, but he was certainly happy.

"People are always pointing out his big nose nowadays," Vi Caldwell said, "but you didn't notice it then because he had his hair swept back. It's only since he's had his hair combed forward that his nose stands out."

Mrs. Caldwell remembers him as a very small boy, small even when he reached manhood. For the record he's five-feet-seven, though he has described himself in "Beatlese" as "two-feet-nine-inches."

This tendency to make perfectly ridiculous, outlandish statements in the style of Edward Lear has always been a Beatle attribute. John Lennon has developed it to perfection, and Paul and George have managed a few good nonsensical put-ons, but Ringo seems to have a delightful knack for the really outrageous, ridiculous phrase and it has never failed to delight teenagers. In fact, this may be one good reason why Ringo is not only the "quiet, miserable and sad" Beatle but also the "popular" Beatle.

Mrs. Caldwell tells of Ringo buying a Vanguard car, the same car he took his wife Maureen home in after those early shows at the Cavern, and before they were married. He had to put a cushion on the driver's seat so that he could see out of the windshield.

In spite of Mrs. Caldwell's memory of Ringo as depressingly quiet, and sad, the girl fans find him "cute." They find, in his awkwardly-put-together features, a "lovable cuteness."

Paul McCartney, commenting on this cuteness, has summed it up with, "If he's cute, it's horrible cute, like an. English bulldog!"

Cute or sad or depressing, Ringo somehow fit in with the other three from the very beginning. If anything, he had more energy and more vitality than the rest, although this doesn't jibe with Mrs. Caldwell's memories.

"I never feel tired after a show," he said. "I'm still leaping around after the others have collapsed and are flopped out and dozing off. I'm afraid this is a habit of mine which annoys them no end.

"Like one night recently, when George was grabbing forty winks between shows, and I went dashing into the dressing room and fell over him. It was his own fault, really, for kipping out on the floor, but he yelled at me, 'Ringo, you ruddy clod! Do you have to leap on my head?'

"I yelled back, 'Well, do you have to sleep on the floor? What are you, a bloomin' dog?'

" 'Yes,' he growled, and bit me in the leg to prove it!"

INSTANT FAME OR, THE ROYAL COMMAND PERFORMANCE

APRIL, 1962, TO OCTOBER, 1963

It is one of the most loosely kept secrets of today's teenagers that John Lennon married his wife when she was pregnant. John himself, with admirable contempt for tradition, has mentioned it a number of times. But the secret has been carefully sidestepped in the fan magazines since a quick comparison of the dates comes up with an eight-month baby—not at all unusual.

The point is that there was no waiting for the marriage. The two had been going together for years and simply considered themselves too young for marriage. When the pregnancy occurred, John, to his credit, did the "right thing" and did it very quickly with no rancor or feeling of "being trapped." They were married August 23, 1962. No parents attended the wedding, but Paul and George both came.

Early marriages of this sort are frowned on in show business, where it is generally accepted that performers are a bit "wild" to begin with, and any early marriage will be followed by early divorce.

Lennon's marriage has lasted over six years so far with no rumor or hint of discord, a situation that one hopes will continue.

The key may lie in Cynthia Lennon, from all accounts a mature and quiet girl. One of the stories given out to the teen magazines is that when John first met her, Cynthia wore her brown hair in a short, curly style. John persuaded her to grow it long and bleach it white-blond, which if nothing else is at least outstanding. Pygmalion-like, the story goes, he has always made her frequent top designers for simple, expensive clothes.

The marriage was kept a secret for as long as possible. Even Rory Storme's mother, a friend of all four boys, wasn't sure. "They used to deny it to everyone, including me," she said. "One night I mentioned that a friend had seen someone very like John at the Register's Office. Paul bounded out of his chair and paced the room shouting, 'He's not married. We keep telling you he's not!' "

What troubled the boys was how the girl fans would react to the news of a Beatle marriage. They were still at the Cavern then, and the crowds of fans were growing. They realized that a great part of their popularity and success hinged on the capricious whims of these children, an irrational breed at best.

When Pete Best left the group, the boys had been denounced and even physically attacked by girl fans. In one of the attacks George had had his eye blackened. Even though he wore it proudly as a sign of his loyalty to Ringo, this had shaken them all up and had taught them that the fans were not to be trifled with.

One of Ringo's girl friends at the time, Paula Bennet, describing a date with Ringo, said, "When we went down in the elevator, he insisted on huddling in a comer, his coat collar pulled up over his face in case anyone recognized him,"

Outside, Ringo waited, flattened in a doorway, while Paula hailed a cab. "I had to ask the driver to pull up slowly outside the club while I held the door open so that Ringo could suddenly dash into the cab without anyone realizing it was him."

George Harrison's brother Harry, talking about those hysterical fans, stated that it was the girls at the Cavern who first whipped up the tremendous fan mania. "After one tour," he said, "the boys were booked to return to the Cavern, and at this announcement fans started queuing up three days in advance of their opening. It was incredible. They were actually camping out there."

When the Beatles heard what was happening they dreamed up a terrific publicity stunt, according to Harry, though it may not have been all publicity. They counted up the number of girls waiting in line, then went down to an all-night coffee stall at Pier Head to buy them pies and sandwiches. They drove back to the Cavern then, and handed the food out.

Harry doesn't believe one of those pies was eaten. "They were probably treasured souvenirs. I know of several girls who took them home and put them on the mantelpiece. A few weeks later one mother had to dust the pie when she cleaned the room!"

It wasn't long before no Beatle was safe after a performance. If there was no secret back way out of the theater, they'd have to make a dash from the front doors.

"Someday," Ringo said at the time, "I'm going to design a theater with an escape hatch, a deep underground tunnel way out to a field and a waiting van."

With this growing fan worship, which the boys recognized as a necessity of success, it's no wonder that they tried to keep John's marriage secret. "They both came to my house to live," his aunt says, describing that period. "And they stayed quite a long time after the baby was born."

The baby was a boy, John Charles Julian Lennon, born April 8, 1963. In those days, Mimi remembers fans hanging around even in the worst rainstorms. "Sometimes they would sit on the doorstep till the early hours of the morning. Some girls would even creep round to the back of the house, and we would suddenly realize that someone was watching us through the window."

It was an incredible situation; the house was closely watched as if it were an espionage-prone military installation. Whenever John was at home Mimi would go through the house lowering curtains. To get him out without running the gauntlet of waiting fans, Mimi would go to the front door and chat with the girls. Word would get out that a Beatle Aunt was talking and they'd all flock to the door from every spy port.

John would then duck out the back, leap over the fence in true silent-movie style, and tear through a neighbor's garden.

"It was really amazing," Mimi says, "that with all this going on the kids never tumbled to it that John was married. After all, with all of it they saw Cynthia coming in and out. Later we even put the baby's pram in the back garden, but the girls never put two and two together ... or maybe they just didn't want to believe that one of their precious Beatles had pulled such a terrible double cross as marriage."

Eventually, of course, they did catch on, and Mimi describes one distraught girl fan screaming at her over the fence, "Is it true? Is it true?"

Mimi answered coldly, "If it is, John will have an earful from me about it."

In the meanwhile the boys kept on at the Cavern, where, slowly, to their way of thinking, their fame and reputation grew. Brian Epstein, in addition to managing them, was culling the Cavern for other properties. He picked up the coatroom girl, Priscilla White, changed her name to Cilia Black for some obscure reason, and began to build her up as a singing star. He also picked up The Big Three, The Fourmost, and the Resno Four. He had already signed Gerry and the Pacemakers, Billy D. Kane, and Tom Quigley, and he was on his way to being a "big time" manager.

But he protested that his big love was, and stayed, the Beatles. They were also his biggest financial investment, and his most successful.

The disorganized clutter of the early engagements began to disappear now as Brian whipped the boys into a smoothly functioning group. Musically,' they worked on their own sound, improving it and smoothing it out. Here Epstein was of no help at all. While he tried to enjoy their music, he realized, and they realized, that he was only trying. Classical music was the only kind he really enjoyed. He appreciated pop music, but only in the sense that he knew its commercial value. It never moved him, and the reaction of the fans was always something of a shock to him.

One of the things that troubled the four Beatles in those days was the unpredictable treatment they received when Epstein wasn't around to protect their interests. On the road they were treated well in some places, but in others pretty shabbily.

In one engagement at Walton, the equipment was set up by Neil by eight o'clock but the boys didn't arrive till nine-thirty when they were due on. They were told rather coldly by the manager that they were an hour late.

They were scheduled to perform for only an hour, but after the last number the manager kept the curtain open and forced them to perform for an extra thirty minutes with, of course, no extra pay. "That'll teach you to arrive late," he told them afterwards.

"He must be joking," Paul said. "It's like being back at school, kept in after lessons."

In retaliation, they didn't show up there for their next date. If they were treated like children, they decided they'd behave like children.

It blew up a minor storm, but fortunately it didn't last ""But this type of treatment as well as these tricks had all disappeared by the time the Beatles had become such a huge success in Liverpool. Liverpool, however, was still a very small puddle. They were hardly known at all in the rest of England. According to Epstein, true Beatlemania didn't descend on the British Isles until October of 1963. It happened suddenly and dramatically," he said, and added, "we weren't prepared for it."

What triggered it was first a smashingly successful concert the boys gave at the London Palladium. It was so successful that they were named for the Royal Variety Show at the Prince of Wales Theatre in London, exactly two years from the date Brian first heard of them, and one year and nine months from the time he first signed them. Up until then the boys had been performing in ballrooms for comparatively small fees, and while the screaming fans were always present, they were far from the hysterical groups that took over after the royal show.

Those were days of strange contrasts. The boys had a reputation, but it was strictly a local one. They were doing well but often as not they were broke. They didn't quite know where they were going, or if they'd ever get there, or if, perhaps, they had already arrived.

Some of the anecdotes Neil and others tell point up the strange ambivalence of those days.

In May of 1963, just five months before the royal performance, Ken Brown, who had played with the three for a while before Pete Best joined them, received a phone call late at night.

Ken was married and living in London by then. As he tells the story, the caller was Neil Aspinall. He told Ken that the boys were in a bit of a jam. They were on the road and due to appear in Sheffield the next night, but they had run out of money. Unless someone helped them out they'd have to sleep in the van overnight. Could Ken lend them twenty pounds?

It was a large sum, and Ken hedged a bit at first, but finally agreed. He and his wife went downstairs to meet the bunch and handed over the money. "They repaid me six weeks later," he said.

It's a hard story to accept, i.e., that just five months before they were the biggest singing sensation in Britain they were so broke that they had to borrow twenty pounds from a friend and then take six weeks before they could pay it back. If the story is true, it's another sign of just how swiftly they climbed to success,

Neil Aspinall's account of a night on the town when the boys were touring is very vivid, and reveals the loneliness they were all beginning to feel.

"When we were on tour," he said, "I was always asked to join the boys on an evening out." According to Neil, this was because he was of the same age and the same background as the Beatles.

"We would usually go out late at night, long after the show had ended and the boys had eaten and changed. It's surprising how many people would offer to open bowling alleys, swimming pools, and the like for the boys' private use in the small hours of the morning."

But it wasn't much fun doing all these things alone.

Most of the time, according to Neil, they would just pile into a car, drive around and look at the town, walking off the tensions of the performance. They were always alone on the road, for none of the boys would allow either wife or girlfriend to accompany them.

Ringo liked to dance, and he would usually end up at a nightclub. The others didn't dance, but if the dance floor was crowded enough, the three would get up and shuffle around with any partners they could find.

Sometimes they would go out to eat after a late show, disgusted with the dreadful monotony of hotel fare. If they drove to a place that was closed, John would get out of the car and walk to the next restaurant while the others drove.

"He loved walking about," Neil said. "Just to prove to himself, I think, that he could still do it. Once in a while people would stop him and ask for his autograph, but he rarely got mobbed. I think a Beatle alone is much safer than all four together."

Safety was becoming a serious problem. The boys were still not important enough to warrant police protection, and yet the growing number of fans was becoming a serious threat. The girls had an unholy urge not only to touch the boys, but to pull off bits of clothing for souvenirs.

Gradually and inevitably the bars of a prison began to' close about the boys. The prison of fame is always more solitary to an entertainer. He has little chance of leading a normal existence, and of all entertainers, singers probably have the least chance of all.

If the singer is a teenage idol, and if he is to be counted a success, he must have a hysterical following of young girls. Yet, just because of this following, he can go nowhere without elaborate preparation and deceptions.

In addition, there is an inevitable narrowing of his circle of friends as the realization arrives, with success, that most of the people he meets are interested only in his success. As a person he becomes lost. He begins to exist only as a personality. Inevitably the personality he must present to the world takes over and what he really is disappears.

How then does the entertainer choose his friends? With whom can he be open and free? Who likes him for himself and not for the personality he has become—or even worse, for the money involved in his success?

Another frustration of this success—in terms of the Beatles—was that now that they had enough money to go wherever they wanted, most places were closed to them because of the fans.

One of the outlets the boys used in rebelling against the prison that success began to put them in was a wild contempt for all the trappings of success. This was based on the belief that if they treated it all casually then it surely couldn't affect them. Like a child who pretends that if something bad doesn't exist it will simply go away.

John Lennon, for example, developed a reputation for being the Beatle who spent the most money, but had no idea of how to handle his financial affairs, as if he were saying, "Look, it's just not that important."

When Aspinall once asked him for money to buy some necessary items, he said he didn't have any with him.

"Well, write a check," Aspinall told him impatiently.

"But I don't even know what bank my money is in. It used to be in the Midland, but I think my accountant changed it." It was not an affectation. He really didn't know, nor did he want to know.

Another method of rebellion was the wild prank or jest. "Look at us. We're not a bit serious about the whole thing." The boys used to clown around, not only on stage but also when they were alone. For example, Neil tells of a one-night stand in a hotel where John and Ringo were dead tired from a long trip, and George was wide awake. To get some sleep they barricaded their door with a wardrobe George, looking for them, tried to get into their room and when the door wouldn't budge he banged and slammed against it till the wardrobe fell to the floor and smashed to bits.

.

As John and Ringo leaped out of bed in amazement, George stood calmly by and said, "What a soft place to put a wardrobe!"

There are dozens of anecdotes like this about the boys' wild behavior, anecdotes that stress their contempt for convention and property. While many of them are press agent's dreams, some few are certainly true, enough to make the point.

In October of 1963, the Beatles headed the bill at the London Palladium while an estimated audience of 15 million watched them on television. This, in everyone's opinion, was the real moment of their arrival at the top.

Only a year before they had cut their first commercial disk. It had taken just one year to springboard them to the top of England's entertainment world, with reverberations that were felt in far-off, unsuspecting America.

For the first time, after the Palladium concert, the London police were called into action to fight more than a thousand screaming teenagers. A motorcycle escort stood by as the boys were rushed to their car.

Describing the scene, a local paper said, "The fans went wild, breaking through a cordon of more than a hundred bobbies and running for the car. They missed it by seconds as it sped away."

The stampede was the end of a fantastic day-long siege at the Palladium. During rehearsals for the evening show, some fifty girls had somehow managed to break through emergency doors. They flooded the stage, swarming around their idols until the police managed to restore order and clear the halls.

And the boys? They had blinked their eyes while they were still wearing tight jeans and leather jackets, dirty shirts and ragged haircuts, pounding out their beat on cheap instruments, and they opened them to a new image, suited, shirted, and tied, stormed by thousands, idolized and hungered after.

Their first reaction was one of terror. "You've never seen the light in the eye of a crowd of stampeding teenagers," George Harrison has said of that day. "You can't know how scary it is to have them grabbing at you and yelling. Sure, it means they love you, but save me from that kind of love. It could eat you right up!"

The boys rallied quickly, however. "They don't worry me," Harrison said later. "In fact I like it. I'd be dead worried if the girls weren't around and the screaming died away."

Ringo, for all his "thickness," probed deeper and came up with something to bolster the boys' images. "It isn't the screaming fans that affect me. That's normal, and anyway; you get used to it. I love "em and it's great to know they love you. But what worries me is the feeling that I might let them down."

John buried his quips and wisecracks and adopted a humble attitude to the situation. "I feel richer and flattered by our good fortune, I am touched by it all."

Paul tried another ploy. "It's fabulous, the success and all that, but I hope people don't begin to think that because we're successful now, we're unapproachable."

This was wishful—or wistful—thinking, the last hope that the prison bars would not be too strong, the lock too unbreakable. But by its very wistfulness it was recognition that the prison bars had already gone up. The boys were irrevocably prisoners of their own fame.

The reactions to the Palladium concert were stunning, and just one week later they were announced for the Royal Command Performance, a recognition by the royal family that was equal to the highest possible approval.

As wild as the reaction to the Palladium concert had been, the reaction to their invitation to the Command Performance was overpowering. When the invitation was issued, the Beatles were playing in a Southport ballroom. Epstein was not around, and there was only Neil and Mal Stevens to fend off a horde of newsmen.

The boys were frankly scared but not at the idea of playing for royalty. "After all," Epstein said later, "the boys were on the way to becoming royalty themselves. Why should they be afraid to play for their own kind?" But they were frightened of the reporters. They were faced, that night, with a solid wall of implacable questions, their first real experience with reporters and the kind of press conference that was later to become a way of life wherever they went.

"I wasn't there at the time," Epstein said, "but the boys were typically loyal to me and said that whatever decision was taken on the royal show would have to be mine."

They didn't get off the hook this easily. The reporters, men and women from Britain's top papers, "pros," were all waiting to tear the boys apart, waiting for some slip of the tongue that they could seize on and blow up out of all proportion. After all, who were these kids, hardly out of their adolescence, to rate a Royal Command?

"Do you think the Beatles from Liverpool should desert their fans by appearing before the boiled shirts and jewels of the privileged in London?"

"Are you going to become swells?"

"Have you forgotten your fans in Liverpool? What are they going to' think?"

"Do you really think you should presume to play for the Queen?"

This was the tenor of questioning and it was all slanted to produce some angry answers, some answers that the reporters could blow up into a fine attack on presumptuous youth. It was deliberate bait for sob columns.

The boys, pale and frightened, looked at the horde of demanding reporters and accepted their first baptism by fire. They listened to the questions, sniffed at the bait, and rejected it.

"Why shouldn't we?" they asked innocently. "She's our Queen too, you know."

And Ringo, grinning blandly, added, "I want to bang the drums for the Queen Mother. Is there anything wrong in that?"

With a laugh that eased the tension, the press agreed that there wasn't, but still, the drift of all the articles they wrote based on that press conference, ran the same way. These are teenage idols. What on earth are the adults doing showing interest in them?

This attitude cropped up for the first time after the Palladium concert, but in later years it became a solid, hostile way of adult thinking. The Beatles and the strange reaction they caused in youth have been viewed with alarm, horror, distaste, and even fear by adults.

It became easy for the papers to blame the Beatles for a lack of taste and control and a dangerous mass hysteria among young people.

But there were a few dissenting voices, even at that time. An English psychologist, Anthony Corbett, actually praised the Beatles, saying, "They provided a desperately needed release for the inhibitions which exist in all of us."

Quoting psychologists or psychiatrists became a favorite newspaper stunt after the invitation to the Command Performance. Dixon Scott, of the London Daily Mirror, dredged up a "well-known-but-nameless psychiatrist" to say, "We are all chaotic and mixed-up inside. We are anxious to have a greater freedom to live. We have a greater need to express ourselves. In the past we have been controlled automatons, but you can't hold nature back forever. We search for outlets and rhythm is one of these outlets. . . ."

The meaning of the Beatle phenomenon had become a national parlor game in England with everyone pro or con, though among the adults it was mostly con.

First the teenagers of Liverpool and then the rest of Great Britain had discovered them, but the British press was reluctant to write about the Beatles. In general the British press will devote all its attention to celebrities who have "made it," but will often ignore anyone on the "way up."

While the Beatles were on the rise, most papers ignored them, but once they hit the big time, once they had a smash success at the Palladium, all the papers sat up and took notice.

Brian Epstein, taking advantage of the press's attention, began rhapsodizing in his releases. "London," he said, "was brought to a standstill by the screaming youth of the south of England. The royal family, the wealthy, and the great were all captivated by the naturalness of the four young men."

Naturalness was the key word as the image of the four young men was forged to the sound of clicking cash registers. These boys must remain unspoiled symbols of youth and honesty.

"As I stood watching from the wings during the Command Performance," Neil Aspinall said, "I knew for a fact that the boys were scared stiff. Paul went out and broke the ice by smiling and saying, 'I'm going to sing a number from The Music Man—which has already been recorded by our favorite American group, Sophie Tucker.'

"Suddenly the highest dignitaries in the land were roaring with laughter. The boys' act stopped the show and the crowning touch came when, after the show, Marlene Dietrich requested the press photographers to shoot her with the Beatles."

Dietrich, eternally young herself, announced, "It was a joy to be with those youngsters. I adore the Beatles."

The Queen Mother found them "young, fresh and vital."

And Princess Margaret, royalty's attempt at its own "young image," was captivated. What more could the boys hope for? What could top this?

TOURING ENGLAND AND THE FALL OF PARIS

OCTOBER, 1963, TO MARCH, 1964

Eight months before the Palladium show, the London Evening Standard had announced that the Beatles were the darlings of Merseyside. The little girls of the part of Liverpool that borders the Mersey River were so "fiercely possessive" about their Beatles, the Standard said, that they forced the local television studio to put them on the air,

How they did this was not clear, but the Standard warned against underestimating the pressure of youth, reporting that Liverpool Beatle fans had threatened not to buy the Beatle's first record, "Please Please Me" lest the boys become so famous they would desert Liverpool and their fans there and go on to fame in London. Fortunately for the Beatles, the Standard also reported enough fans still loyal enough to buy five hundred thousand records in one week.

Even allowing for the press agent's fine hand in this story, there is enough truth in it to be impressive.

What it was that attracted these youngsters to the Beatles no one knew, but everyone was willing to guess. "I think it's their looks that starts the girls queuing up out-side the Liverpool Grafton at 5:30 for the 8 P.M. show," reporter Maureen Cleaves guessed.

These were the Beatles after Epstein had polished the up a bit, and Cleaves goes on to give an amusing account of what they looked like then. Even with Epstein's refinements, she noted that they looked "scruffy, but scruffy on purpose. They wore bell-bottomed suits of a rich burgundy color, with black velvet collars and pink shirts." These are neither the earlier Beatles nor the later, but some image in-between, now lost forever in time. She pointed out that "of course they wore boots," and they had "French hairstyles."

The youth of Liverpool came, saw and imitated. Liverpool lads of twelve and up began to wear small bouffant Beatle cuts with the fringe brushed forward.

Onstage, the boys showed an extraordinary awareness of their own ability, bursting with self-confidence and professional polish. Their patter between songs was in the music hall tradition with slightly bawdy schoolboy overtones.

A Liverpool housewife described them, at this point in their career, as "Beat-up and depraved in the nicest possible way." She also felt that they were very friendly and charming and appeared not only to like each other, but to like everyone else as well.

Even at this time the boys wore their defensive attitude against the Establishment proudly and accented their contempt for the trappings of success.

In a press interview John Lennon said, "We all want to' get rich so we can retire. We don't want to go straight, or get to be all-around entertainers."

In an out-and-out bid for the money to be found in movie making, he said, "We'd also like to have a bash at acting. Not that we can do it, but we'd like to see ourselves up there anyway."

When asked what their music was, just what the Mersey sound, the Liverpool beat signified, John threw up his hands in despair. "People try to pin labels on us. Now they say we're rhythm and blues, but ever since I read, two years ago, that calypso was taking England by storm, I've never believed a word I've read. I think your readers are all like me and wouldn't believe a word I said about our music. For us it's just good fun."

As a putdown, Paul McCartney added that in his opinion John Lennon was self-confident because he was too blind to see all the nasty little faces in the audience, faces not enjoying their singing at all.

"He can't see a thing without his glasses anyway, and he's too conceited to wear them. He makes up all those catch phrases like, 'Thank you, folks. You're too kind.' Imagine saying that twenty times over!"

When asked about the Beatle humor, Paul considered seriously, and then said, "Our humor is based on anything other people don't laugh at, death for instance, or disease.

It sounds dreadful if you write it down, but cruelty, that really makes everyone laugh.

"We're not being unkind," he elaborated "We're just silly."

And silly they were for the next eight months, but it was a silliness that paid off in a ballooning popularity.

The queue-ups that developed during those days of growing Beatle popularity were really no new thing on the

Liverpool scene. In 1957, when the Cavern Club opened up— patterned after the famous Parisian jazz club, Le Caveau—it only had room for six hundred people, even standing, and yet on opening night, before any Beatle had yet made his appearance, 2,000 people queued up outside.

But the Beatle Queue, as it came to be called, was a queue to outqueue all others. It would sometimes start three days in advance. The waiting fans would bring along as many of the comforts of home as they could manage—camp cots, blankets, portable stoves, transistors—all through the latter part of autumn and even into winter, and an English winter at that!

Describing one of these queues, the British Daily

Telegraph said, "It looked more like a death watch than the prelude to a joyous Beatle event." They went on to describe the side effects of Beatle queuing. "Three ambulances, rarely short of patients, some of them schoolgirls, dealt with more than one hundred cases of fainting or exhaustion. Several were treated at hospital.

Seventy-four police were on duty, and special checkpoints had to be set up."

Here, for the first time, we begin to get an idea of the dreadful problem the police faced in keeping order as this new mania grew. Again the papers began to groan aloud.

"Police at Newcastle-upon-Tyne struggled with screaming teenagers fighting to get tickets for the Beatle 'pop' group.

Clashes between police and teenagers were frequent,"

At Hull, 8,000 young people waited in line for three days. There were only 5,000 available tickets, and once these were sold 3,000 teenagers found they had waited for nothing. A police officer labeled the riot that followed "an incredible experience. There has never been anything like it."

The queuing and the wild howling fans actually started before the Royal Command Performance. Shortly after Palladium success, the boys had left England to tour Sweden for eight days. Their records were now flooding the airwaves, as BBC and a growing number of European stations devoted more and more time to their music. Then fans too grew to fearful numbers.

They arrived back in England on the thirty-first of October to find the airport flooded with screaming teenagers.

At one of the performances at Southport, 2,000 screaming fans, many of them wearing imitations of the Beatles' jackets, packed the hall to capacity. Some of these fans had queued since 9 A.M. of the day before to be sure of getting a ticket.

"Very well-behaved," was an awestruck police comment on the teenagers' line-up. "We have had no disturbance of any kind."

However, well-behaved or not, half an hour after the Beatles went onstage they had to be smuggled out of a side entrance to the hall, sneaked into a waiting van, and driven home in secrecy.

One of the peculiar offshoots of the boys' growing prominence was the sudden popularity of places with which they had once been associated. After the Beatles' first visit to America, the school which John and Paul had attended had dozens of requests for pen pals from American girls.

After the Palladium show, the Cavern Club took on all the aspects of a sacred shrine, lacking only a number of crutches hanging outside to attest to a few miracles.

The Chief Information Officer of Liverpool, Mr. Reg Millington, said of this strange affection for places associated with the boys, "there has been a steady flow of requests for information about hotels and 'digs' from young people, mostly girls, who want to make a Mecca-like pilgrimage to visit the Cavern Club and other places the

Beatles have been associated with.

"It seems that if you can go back to your own jazz club and say, 'I've been to the Cavern Club where it all started,' you are assured of a certain important status."

When asked how he handled these requests, Mr. Millington said he simply sent the youngsters Liverpool's official illustrated travel brochure, marking the Cavern's location and the location of certain select hotels.

"What they don't realize is that they must be members of the Cavern Club before they can get in, and I tell them they will probably have to pay an extra charge."

During the mad and frantic days between the Palladium show and the Command Performance, the boys received, with a kind of inevitability, a bid to make a motion picture, and at the end of October they had signed a contract to film a major production backed by United Artists. The script was to be written by a prize-winning Liverpool playwright, Alun Owen, and it was to be produced by Walter Shenson, the man credited with making an international star out of Peter Sellers.

Since Sellers was something of an idol to the boys, the choice of Shenson seemed just perfect to them. Everything began, in fact, to be "just perfect" or "gear," a word from the local Liverpool vernacular which meant just about anything good. The Beatles, in fact, have managed in the past five years to put the word "gear" into every American, English, and Australian teenager's vocabulary, and not as an automobile part.

The film, planned for black-and-white production, was scheduled to start shooting in February. By now their fame was so great that it was decided that they would play themselves in the movie instead of fictional characters.

This also meant that no real story had to be constructed, and the whole thing could be rushed into production as soon as possible, at least while the boys were still riding the crest of their popularity. No one could conceive of this popularity lasting longer than a few more months.

"We haven't decided on anything yet in the way of script or locale," Alun Owen announced, "but I'm delighted with the idea. It just happens I'm mad about the Beatles anyway. They are so full of life. In fact, if anything, this love for life will be the theme, the exuberant theme of our movie."

The Beatles came back from Stockholm and their eight days of touring to find themselves not only famous as a musical group, but potential movie stars.

"They couldn't believe any of it was happening," Ep" stem said. "They were like four kids caught in the cookie jar and praised for their cunning. They couldn't help but feel a bit guilty, especially Ringo. He felt he had walked into this unknowingly, and it had all exploded around him."

The Command Performance was almost a letdown, but thanks to the excitement of the fans it became very real.

"Fingers protecting their eyes, they burst into the Prince of Wales Theatre in London, inches ahead of two hundred screaming teenage fans," the Liverpool Echo said.

And this was only the rehearsal! A horde of fans had been in wait since 8 A.M., camped out at the two entrances, and even fifty policemen were almost helpless to handle them.

Ones inside the theater, the Beatles were in a stage of real siege, with their freedom limited to the corridor between the dressing room and the stage.

Even this slim freedom was taken from them when the reporters descended. "Are you nervous?" they were asked again and again.

John Lennon answered honestly, "There won't be many in the audience, about a thousand, and we've certainly played before many more than that, but it's the people, who they are, that makes us nervous."

George Harrison said, "We're not only nervous, we're really blockaded in here. We'll have to eat in. We can't possibly go out." With a laugh, "I expect they'll send in some dog biscuits."

Paul McCartney told the reporters, "It's a very select audience. My Dad's here tonight—in his evening dress too."

"He's selling the ice cream," Ringo explained.

"But only to the Royal box," George added, and said, "This is really our day off, but we always spend it like this. It keeps us in trim."

And this whole exchange with the reporters was only a few days after their baptism by fire in their first real press conference. The boys were adapting to fame with unnerving swiftness.

The Royal Variety Show over, the four boys started a tour of England. During this tour their fifth single record, "I Want to Hold Your Hand," became the Number One best seller in Great Britain, and their first long-playing album was issued with the best advance sales of any record in the world up to that date.

On November 12th, the same day that "I Want to Hold Your Hand" was released, the Beatles' concert in Portsmouth Guildhall was canceled because Paul McCartney came down with gastric influenza.

A crowd of several hundred youngsters, mainly girls, shouted for the Beatles frantically outside the Guildhall. They couldn't bear the idea of the show being canceled. Many of the girls wept, and some collapsed hysterically and had to be rushed off in ambulances or comforted by the police.

Three hours before the curtain was due to rise, the Beatles arrived at the Guildhall by car, with Paul determined to go on, for "his fans' sake."

However, before they could even get started on the rehearsal, Paul collapsed with a temperature over 100 degrees.

Paul's illness was their press agent's gain. He immediately contacted the manager of the Guildhall, who adopted a cloak-and-dagger style to announce to the waiting fans, "The Beatles have been spirited away to a small Southsea hotel which shall remain nameless."

"Paul McCartney is a very sick boy at the moment,' Neil Aspinall told the press. "A doctor will be seeing him in the morning, and a decision about the rest of the tour will be made then."

Crowds of girls gathered around the Guildhall, solemnly waiting for bulletins on their Beatle. These came slowly through the night, straight from the Beatles' new press agent's typewriter.

And so it went through the fans' endless night, till the morning broke with the grateful news that Paul was out of danger and would recover. The girls wept.

The collapse had one repercussion. The Beatles were due the next day at Southern Television's Studios at Southampton, and a rumor had started around that a kidnapping of the four was planned by university students as a "rag day stunt."

Stunt or public-relations brainstorm, forty police were rushed to the studios, and four television announcers were disguised as Beatles, hair and all, to act as decoys. The stunt never came off because Paul's illness prevented the boys from arriving is Southampton on schedule, and evidently no one wanted to kidnap the television announcers.

A few days later, American television was invited into the act, and CBS and NEC were given full permission to film the Beatles at the Winter Garden Theatre in Bourne-mouth.

The manager of the Winter Garden made a big noise about bringing in giant steaks for the boys in case they were besieged by fans and couldn't leave the theater.

What happened to the steaks and the American television plans is not known. Presumably, both fell somewhere along the way, but the publicity survived.

Four days in advance of the start of sales at the Odeon cinema in London, nine young girls began to queue up for a show to be held on December 8th, more than three weeks away. Meanwhile George Harrison, like Paul was sicken with a severe case of gastric flu, but rallied to make the next show with the boys.

Paul, wan, but with chin so high his eyes were bidden by his bangs, told a press conference, "The Beatles will break under the strain of this tour!" The boys were testing the rudiments of public relations.

"In Germany," Paul elaborated, "we worked seven hours a night, seven days a week, and this does not seem much of a strain after that."

However, after the show, the boys escaped from the fans through an underground tunnel a hundred yards long, a tunnel which led from the hall to a point twenty yards away from the theater, at which point it came up to street level.

On December 13th they finished the exhausting British tour in time to plunge into rehearsals for a Christmas show. This was presented in Bradford, Liverpool, and London, and then, for a brief period, the boys relaxed and caught their breath, concentrating on escaping fans on their own home ground.

"But we're used to doing it here," John Lennon reassured the press. "After all, we know the terrain and we can get away through our private escape holes. It's not so bad."

Before this first British tour had started, a journalist had told Brian Epstein, "By Christmas it will be impossible to look at the front page of any newspaper in England without seeing some reference to the four Beatles."

"He was right," Epstein said. "We became, all of us, overexposed. At first the sight of the Beatles in the newspapers, the discussion of their views, their hobbies, their clothes, was all exciting. They liked it, and to tell the truth, so did I. It was good for them, and of course it was also good for business."

But in spite of this, Epstein began to worry and the worry grew worse. Were the people seeing too much of the boys? Would they eventually become sick and tired of Beatles this and Beatles that, of literally having their faces rubbed in the Beatles again and again. Perhaps he should concentrate more on foreign tours where they weren't too exposed. Perhaps the U.S.A. or France.

Epstein arranged for their first French tour. It would take some of the pressure off England. After all, how much could the English public take?

An awful lot, it seemed!

By the winter of 1963, everyone was clamoring to be identified in some way with at least one of the four Beatles. "If you had a Beatle at a party you were 'made' socially," Epstein said.

That was England as they took off for Paris in the first month of 1964. But Paris was another matter and fifty million Frenchmen, if not wrong, were at least indifferent.

When the Beatles arrived at Le Bourget airport there were forty curious newsmen from the French newspapers, but not even one fan. It was a terrible blow. The boys felt as if they had stepped out of Wonderland back into the harsh, cruel light of the real world.

Worse was still to come. At the Olympia Theater, where they were to open, the tickets hadn't even been sold out.

However, Brian went to work furiously, hired French press agents, flooded the newspapers with releases, and wined and dined the French columnists, begging them to do anything, even attack the Beatles if necessary, but at least mention them. After the tour he was able to announce proudly, "By the end of three weeks there were wailing, chanting mobs surging around the theater, and hundreds of club-wielding gendarmes were on nightly patrol." This was more like the Beatle image.

Epstein boasted that by the end of the tour Paris stores were filled with Beatle wigs, and the songs of the Beatles were heard in the land— blasting over the loudspeaker systems m most of the stores.

"Paris fell," he said proudly. "Later, dramatically, America fell too, and in the summer Copenhagen, Amsterdam, and the whole of Australasia."

Back from their successful storming of Paris, the four boys flew across the Atlantic to conquer America and appear on success' pinnacle, the phlegmatic Mr. Sullivan's show.

They conquered sad-faced Sullivan, and legend has it that he actually smiled at them twice, each time the Neilsen ratings bubbled over.

In March, after a triumphant return to England, they started shooting A Hard Day's Night—though at that time it wasn't called that. It remained for Ringo to have the honor of titling it and stealing the show.

UNDERSTANDING THE BEATLEMANIACS

NOVEMBER, 1963, TO FEBRUARY, 1964

How the Beatles conquered New York City during their first visit in February of 1964 was described in the prologue. It was love at first sight, at least on the part of the teenagers, but there had been intimations of the love affair long before the Beatles came to our shores.

As early as November 15, 1963, Time magazine discovered the four and, to America's delight, quoted the famous Beatle witticism of John Lennon, made during the Command Performance in London's Prince of Wales Theatre.

"Those in the cheaper seats clap," Lennon called out. "The rest of you rattle your jewelry." In a less confident mood, Lennon said, "The day the fans desert us, I'll be wondering how I'll pay for my whiskey and cokes." He went on to admit that in his own opinion, they had little else to offer the world but their ability to arouse screaming hysteria in a limited age-segment of the population. The years since have proved him completely wrong.

In spite of this low self-estimate, or perhaps because of it, the Beatles were living a basically simple life. "We're not interested in living it up," Ringo said. "All our money goes into Beatles Ltd. and we take out only enough for clothes and a few ciggies."

At that time, the time of their first visit to New York, their money, though nowhere near what it is now, was still considerable. They were earning about eighteen hundred pounds a week playing one-night stands all over Britain, and their records were selling over 2,500,000 copies. A month later, Epstein estimated the sales at over 5,000,000.

Describing their music before they arrived here, Time magazine said, "The raucous, big beat sound they achieve by electric amplification makes a Beatle performance slightly orgiastic, but the boys are the very spirit of good clean fun."

They were described as shaggy Peter Pans with mushroom haircuts and high white shirt collars.

The New Yorker magazine discovered them a month after Time, a month before their first visit, and admitted that their appearance was distinctive. It saw them as "ancient British" in style and described their clothes as lapel-less suits patterned after a Pierre Cardin design.

While Time heard their songs as mainly "Yeh! screamed to the accompaniment of three guitars and a thunderous drum," The New Yorker was more perceptive. "Their music is marked by a strong rhythm that has come to be known variously as the Liverpool Sound and the Mersey Beat."

Brian Epstein, three months before his protégés arrived in New York to take the city by storm, altered their image again for a press interview.

"They have a tremendous style and a great effervescence," he told reporters. "Their beat is something like rock and roll, but different. They are not phony. They are genuine. They have life, humor, and strange, handsome looks."

Admitting that they were called a working-class phenomenon, he still insisted that their appeal was classless. "Mummies like the Beatles too. They think they are sweet. They approve.

"I think America is ready for the Beatles," Epstein concluded, and he was quite right. America was indeed ready, in fact overready.

When the four Beatles finally flew back to England and the bewildered adults of New York City shook their heads and popped their ears and tried to sort things out, a multitude of explanations for the popularity of the Beatles sprang up.

According to the author of The Hidden Persuaders, Vance Packard, who was Madison Avenue's own "jaundiced eye on advertising," the Beatles filled some important subconscious need of teenagers. Packard theorized that youngsters see themselves as a subjugated people, constantly exposed to abrupt edicts from the adult world.

The entertainment universe offered a sense of escape to these young people, especially when it publicized some teen star's parental defiance. The Beatles, however, he noted, could not hope to outdo Elvis Presley in appalling children's parents. Instead they substituted an "amiable impudence and a generalized disrespect for just about everybody."

The Beatles had also, Packard said, filled other subconscious teenage needs. In their new image—shades of Pierre Cardin—they were no longer roughnecks, but loveable, cuddly imps who had succeeded in bringing out the mother instinct in girls. [Epstein: "Mummies like them!"]

Of course, this interpretation, while clever, is open to some raised eyebrows. If the hysterical, "orgiastic" reaction of the girls who watched the Beatles and listened to their music is motherly, then Oedipus be damned.

Mr. Packard got down to reality, however, when he noted that the four boys managed to take adolescent girls clear out of this world. In the darkened auditorium they could let all inhibitions go and "cut loose" in a primitive sense. "They can retreat from rationality and individuality. Mob pathology takes over."

But the auditorium is rarely that dark, and much of the same action takes place, or took place, in front of home television sets. While it's true that the girls experienced a hysterical release, it may not have been as great as Mr. Packard suggested.

He got much closer to the truth, to a real understanding of the whole bit when he noted that the Beatles were different, and peculiarly the teenager's own. He concluded, on an optimistic note, that surliness was out, exuberance in, pomposity out, humor in.

Nobody can deny, then or now, that the Beatles were exuberant and punctured pomposity with their own solid humor.

Alan Brien, a young English critic, tried, in the summer that followed their visit, to explain the Beatles and Beatlemania to American readers of Mademoiselle Magazine. More observant Americans, possibly because he is closer to the Beatles' origin, Mr. Brien made a number of clever points,

Refuting the possibility that the four boys were "phallic symbols," Mr. Brien pointed out that what the teenagers were obsessed with was not important. "We don't study a shoe to understand a shoe fetishist," he said. What mattered was that the impact of the Beatles was the same as if they were wisecracking royalty. Like any members of royalty, they needn't justify their existence. It was sufficient that they existed.

It was also possible, he speculated further, that they were deliberately created or designed to incite teenage idolatry, that they were manufactured idols for the teenage market.

Brian Epstein vehemently denied that they were manufactured artists. "Why shouldn't they be where they are?" he asked. "They make a nice sound."

Denying that they had any tricks or gimmicks (electric amplification in all fairness is now considered neither tricky nor gimmicky, nor is studio mixing of sound tracks looked on as unusual), he claimed that their charm lay in their naturalness.

"What's wrong with a good scream?" Mr. Epstein asked. To explain how helpful it could be he told the story of a screaming youngster at one of the Beatles' concerts who dropped her purse, stopped screaming long enough to pick it up and put it in a safe place, and then resumed her screaming.

"That's not hysteria," he pointed out quite justly. "That's self-expression."

Perhaps it was self-expression, and if so the answer to the Beatles' attraction for teenagers may lie in Mr. Brien's statement in Mademoiselle that the study of a shoe fetishist lies not in the study of a shoe, but in the fetishist himself. The true understanding of Beatlemania may lie not in understanding the Beatles, but in understanding the maniacs.

Why did the girls respond the way they did? What did they get out of it? What did it mean to them?

This is a most difficult area to explore, especially since the girls most affected were only twelve or thirteen at the time, an age at which articulate exploration of their own psyches is not an easy thing. In retrospect, many, having reached a more mature age, have looked back and tried to understand what the Beatles meant to them.

A girl who was fourteen years old at the time, a parochial school freshman and one of Long Island's "top ten" Beatle fans, felt it was mostly the ability to identify with them. "You know, the Beatles had their tea at four in the afternoon. Well, when it's four over there, it's ten over here, so every night at ten we had our tea, my cousin and I. And they had jam and toast with it, so we did too. We ate this jam from Liverpool." The fact that she had her time zones backwards didn't seem to bother her sense of sharing.

In this girl the urgent need to identify with the boys, to be close to them, oddly enough went with pride in being a nonconformist. "I think you should stand out in a crowd. I think you should be yourself."

But the whole thing was more than a matter of identification with the Beatles. Another teenager, older and more articulate, eighteen at that time, has refuted the suggestion that the reaction of the girls was based on their parents' disapproval.

"It was the adults who turned against the Beatles just because the kids loved them," she said.

In reminiscing about her own involvement, she said, "I saw them at the concert from up front. I wasn't one of the screamers. In fact, I had promised myself I wouldn't scream when they came on, and I didn't, but my eyes filled with tears. There was something about them, an animal magnetism. I wanted to scream. I wanted to turn to the adults and say, 'See, this is ours.' I left and it hurt. I couldn't get enough of them. It was an answer to something, to some real need I don't even understand."

Another girl, younger then, said, "Oh, it was sexual, what we felt. Not overtly so, not blatant, the way Elvis Presley was, but still— Why we used to talk about it, and we'd say it would be all right to go to bed with one of the Beatles, but not with anyone else. We were average kids, all virgins, but the Beatles—well, they woke us up. If we weren't sexually aroused, they aroused us."

Another girl, fifteen at the time, agreed. "It was a real physical thing. They satisfied a tremendous need, and yet going to see them made you more frustrated."

"Were you carried away in spite of yourself," one girl screamer was asked, "or did you scream because the other girls screamed?"

"Neither, really. I think it was because all the screaming allowed me to do it. Once I started, I wasn't aware of the others around me. I was alone. I reacted alone."

"Some of the girls tore off their clothes," a seventeen year old said. "There was a feeling in the air. You could touch it. The beat, it was very different, sexual, the beat, the tune, the rhythm. It wasn't rock 'n' roll. Rock 'n' roll is banged out. This wasn't."

Another white girl made a racial distinction. "Up till then the Negroes had cornered the market on music. They were on top of the heap. We all knew they were best. Now here were four white boys who had them licked. I think that meant something to us."

"Did you want to meet them?" the girls were asked, and there was complete unanimity on that point. "No!" To see them, yes. To meet them, no. "We wanted to worship them in a way, to idolize them, but you can't meet an idol. It just wouldn't be right. Why? Well for one thing, he wouldn't be an idol anymore."

A girl who was thirteen at the time said, "I was excited. The excitement all around me welled up in me. I sat through the other acts, enduring them, but when they came on I began to cry."

Another girl, a girl who was only twelve when she first heard the Beatles, has made a point of saying, "The Beatles were far enough away for me to dream happily about them. I knew, and even subconsciously hoped, they would never enter my world."

But the Beatles, she feels, belonged to her age group. "They were something our parents didn't understand, and we were glad of that. We just didn't want them to like the Beatles. I don't think we were rebelling, just trying to prove to them, to our parents, that we too had something great."

About the screaming, she admits freely that she was one of the screamers. "Screaming over the Beatles was fun. I knew perfectly well it was only a television screen that I was seeing them on, but I had to show Ringo that I loved him. He and the rest had so much more charm than the average crew-cut baseball-playing American boy."

Now, at sixteen, she feels that she has toned down a bit. "My mother will listen to a Sinatra record while she cleans the house, and she'll smile with a certain nostalgic air. I don't think it will be long before I'll do the same while listening to the Beatles."

In an attempt to understand the male reaction to the Beatles, a group of seventeen and eighteen-year-old college boys were brought together for a bull session. All of them had been Beatle fans in 1964.

Again and again the talk was pulled back to, "How did they affect you? What did they do to you? How did you react? What did you feel?" And just as often the boys eased out of any direct comment on this level and tried to intellectualize their emotions.

"It was their originality, their creativity that grabbed me. I felt that they brought a conscience to pop music."

"We felt that the girls were too emotional. Oh, we identified, to an extent—why today's long hair in boys is a result of the Beatles."

"Yes, it's the type of image they projected, opposed to the football type. That was what got us."

"But they've gone beyond their image. Their whole attitude conveyed a spirit kids liked to identify with. They were always kidding around, they were exotic, strange, lively, and most of all, disrespectful."

"But their songs were good too, the music was fresh melodically, not very deep, but there was something universal about it."

"I liked their music, but I couldn't take their image. All the hysteria!"

"But they were authentic. I wouldn't call their music great, but it was creative. You just knew they were trying to say something."

"I thought all the screaming was ridiculous. Like with Sinatra and Benny Goodman, my folks screamed at them, and Presley. It was a fad. We had it before and it'll probably happen again."

"I don't know. I think it was electrifying even listening to' their records, even though I couldn't scream or get excited. I felt too sophisticated for that; but what I liked was their disrespect for authority, you know, they opened a whole new avenue for rebellion."

"More than that, more than that—you know, they came here first after the assassination. I think they replaced Kennedy as a hero for youth."

HARD DAY'S NIGHT AND AN EASY TOUR

JULY, 1964, TO SEPTEMBER, 1964

On Monday night, July 6, 1964, *A Hard Day's Night* opened at the London Pavilion Theatre. The film critic of the London Times admitted, the next day, that the film was not, by any manner of means, the usual sort of thing film makers come up with to exploit the latest show business sensation.

And indeed the film wasn't. The insipid motion pictures ground out by the Hollywood film mills to star Elvis Presley, Pat Boone, or Fabian are stereotyped scripts with stock boy-meets-girl plots and serve only as celluloid cement to hold a number of tunes together. A Hard Day's Night bore no resemblance to this type of film. For one thing it was rough and grainy, choppy and New Wave in its editing, quite obviously handheld in its camera work and as far from "professional slickness" as it could get. Instead of the sickeningly sweet effect of the Hollywood film, it dazzled and deafened the viewer.

The picture took everyone, critics and fans alike, by surprise. The boys clowned and japed their way through it, and brought to the film their own peculiar brand of insanity and mockery. They held the "whole ruddy mess" up for people to look at, and if you were brave enough not to flinch, it was all worth seeing. In the end the picture became a means of projecting their own image, four boys in adult bodies thumbing their noses at the world.

Musically, the London Times said, "several of the numbers are treated as contrapuntal sound track accompaniments to screen action of quite another sort." It labeled the screen action goonish humor, but noted that it gave a vivid glimpse of backstage show business life.

The main trouble with the film was that too many bright ideas and pictures were flung at the viewer one after another, with no breathing space and hardly any quiet footage to get one's breath back before the next onslaught.

The four boys were wise enough not to try to act, but they bounced their way through the film in their own image and they managed very well to project their separate and genuine personalities.

The story of the film, boiled down to a sentence, is a hectic day in the life of a pop group who just happen to be called John, Paul, George, and Ringo. In the course of the day the boys cavort to a good selection of tunes, some old some new, but all written by John and Paul.

Acting themselves was probably the best thing the four boys could have done, because that was precisely what all the fans went to see: the Beatles playing the Beatles. What the boys managed to project, aside from their own images, was a pointed mockery of the Establishment, always in a low-key, offhand manner that made it all the more effective.

One of the highlights of the movie was a bit with Ringo where in an old droopy raincoat and cloth cap he deserts the group for a while and goes on a sad pilgrimage of broken-down bomb sites and pallid pubs.

Another highlight came when the four capered through a deserted playground to the musical accompaniment of one of their own songs. It turns into a magnificent bit of cinema.

A little more than a month after the London opening, the film opened in New York City at a number of theaters simultaneously, a clever device to increase the attendance at preview showings. The rabid teenage audience guaranteed a sellout in every theater, to the accompaniment to shrieks and sighs.

Most New York reviewers agreed that producer Walter Shenson, director Richard Lester, and writer Alun Owen had all done well by the boys. Owen, particularly, was signaled out for a fine, sly job of kidding the Beatles, their type of music, TV programs, the public, the police, and photographic nuts, in that order.

What the reviewers missed was that the boys themselves had done the greater part of the kidding with that ad-lib quality so much their own. The trio of producer-director-writer was mainly responsible for capturing this Beatlesque quality, not for creating it,

The New York Herald Tribune took a deep look at the film and saw the four shaggy-haired boys taking part in "an eggheaded picture, lightly scrambled, a triumph of the Beatles and the bald."

The picture "jumps from the start," reviewer John Molleson said, and "the boys can't sing nearly as well as they can't act. But they are themselves, and that is enough."

Labeling it a "doubtful documentary" he protests that the "beat, beat, beat of the Beatles for eighty-five minutes has the impact of Ravel's Bolero."

Molleson found the camera work filled with fantasy and charm, the gags funny and furious, the surrealist shots imaginative and different.

But most important, the film struck Molleson as an exposure of the personalities of the four. And with some surprise, he found the personalities likable.

The New York Times' Bosley Crowther also loved the picture, calling it a "whale of a comedy." He went on to say it tickles the intellect. "It is much more sophisticated in theme and technique than its seemingly frivolous matter promises."

The Villager, called the Beatles themselves an "authentic expression of our times, a social phenomenon so radical and revolutionary, so intense and widespread, that they cannot be dismissed as a publicity stunt." Labeling the film a "great one" it rhapsodized about the Beatles' talent as comedians, putting it on the "level of genius."

Also on the intellectual front, Andrew Sams in The Village Voice hesitated to speculate on the meaning of the Beatles, but after a proper pause went on to say that "they express effectively a great many aspects of modernity which have converged inspiredly in their personalities."

It's not the way the boys would have put it, but the stressing of modernity is very interesting. The boys are modem beyond denial. They are the new wave, the new sound, the put-on and, as we now realize some four years later, the dropout. They synthesize and epitomize today, and this is perhaps the real key to their appeal to youth.

Newsweek called the film "surprisingly palatable." In this, as in every other review, there is an element of patronizing surprise. "Whoever would have thought it?" The surprise is understandable; the patronization is symbolic of everything divisive between adult and teen. Who in the adult world would have thought the film would become a success, just as who in the teen world would have doubted for a moment that it would be anything but a smashing success? It is a clearcut example of the generation gap.

It is also interesting to. adults to see this gap being crossed by the movie itself, the first real instance in our time of a crossover, of an awareness in the adult world that this group of four boys emitted more than a hard-to-hear noise.

Aside from the generation gap, there was also a nation-to-nation gap in the acceptance of A Hard Day's Night. An item from a Paris paper on October 30th of that year points out that the film had a hard day and a hard night in Paris. It was pulled out of the only theater showing it after four weeks and an extremely low attendance.

The Frenchmen, however, may have been wrong, for by May of 1966, when it was pretty well played out, the film was estimated to have made a profit of 2 million dollars for United Artists Corporation, more than three times the cost of making the film.

During the filming of *A Hard Day's Night,* George Harrison met a young would-be actress named Patti Boyd. A teenage magazine, looking down its nose, pointed out that Miss Boyd had not been a Beatle fan when she was picked to be one of the girls in A Hard Day's Night.

"But it was only a matter of weeks before she became a big fan of George's," the magazine added coyly. "She's a dolly girl and a successful model," they reassured their readers, "and she's even more attractive in person than she is in photos.

"Patti's not really the domesticated type," the magazine worried. "She likes her evenings out with George, though she's more fond of dancing than he is, but she is eager to please him."

Amid a lot of this silly chatter, the magazine tried to explain in its "serious vein" why neither Patti nor any other Beatle girls go along on tours. "It's just not safe for the girls to go with them. The boys travel between six and seven hundred miles a day, get mobbed by thousands of desperate fans, perform before frantic audiences, go to official receptions and are asked to visit the sick, and sign never-ending stacks of autograph books—there just isn't time for anything else, on tour."

Patti Boyd, just twenty, joined the growing inner circle of Beatle people and a year later became Mrs. Harrison. It is fascinating to see how this inner circle grew, as the bars separating the boys from the rest of the world grew stronger and closer together. More and more the boys, shut off from the outside microcosm, worked on the creation of their own microcosm.

It was about this time that John Lennon, who had been doodling and scribbling for years, was persuaded that it might be a profitable venture to turn out a book of comic essays, poetry, and sketches. He had, after all, more or less attended, an art college, and theoretically he could draw. He was verbal and witty enough to be a writer and had an inhumanly wild addiction to puns.

The book, which "wrote very quickly," came to less than one

hundred pages, even stretched out, and the publishers took it on gratefully because anything done by a Beatle, about a Beatle, or for a Beatle had to be successful.

What stunned the publishers and those in-the-know was the enthusiastic reception of John's book. *Called In His Own Write,* the title pun was mild and inconspicuous ide some of those perpetrated in the text. A sampling of quotes show the style used by Lennon. "All of a surgeon . . . the gift of gob . . . putting it lithely . . ."

But more than punning, Lennon's writing takes words and phrases as they sound to the muddy Liverpool ear, and reproduces them without mercy for the English language, as you can see by phrases like, "all aboard speeching . . . deep breathing is Nescafe for a dark voice . . . deep breeding and in haley is very impotent for broadcast ... I sat be lonely down a tree ... to make an honest womb of her . . ."

There is a madness in the writing along with a witty insanity that impelled the London Daily Mail to credit John with "an original, infernal machine of a mind," while the London Times Literary Supplement, a quiet publication, shook its head in disbelief, but admitted that the book was worth the attention of anyone who fears "for the impoverishment of the English language and the British imagination."

Both prose and poetry mingle more-than-free association with pun after pun, and to illustrate the odd mélange there are drawings by Lennon that seem a cross between Virgil Partch and James Thurber—with Hugh Lofting's absolute lack of draftsmanship—yet withal, possessing a perfectly whimsical charm.

This was Lennon in his own write—and rather well-writ.

With this under John's belt, and the film of A Hard Day's Night put away in the can, the boys took themselves off for a triumphant spring and early summer tour that included Denmark and Holland, Hong Kong, Australia and New Zealand.

In Hong Kong, Brian Epstein noted that the "phlegmatic Chinese were overwhelmed by the Beatles," and when the group arrived in Adelaide, Australia, in response to a petition signed by 80,000 townspeople, nearly a third of a million citizens lined the Anzac Highway from the airport to the city's center, cheering and applauding, waving flags and throwing streamers and flowers in the path of the Beatles' car.

The Australian crowds were the largest, but certainly the friendliest on the tour, according to Brian, who promptly told a story to contradict this. One unfriendly young man took a dislike to Ringo's long hair. He backed up his feelings with action, and lunged forward through a cheering crowd of Aussies to grab at Ringo's head.

"He was jabbed smartly in the ribs by the elbow of an otherwise nonviolent Beatle-minder, and later complained that he had been attacked. A typical performance," Brian said. "No matter where they went the boys were never safe from attacks of this sort. It's no wonder that they tended to draw away from crowds more and more, until eventually touring became not only a dangerous and deadly occupation, but a hateful one as well. Can anyone blame them for finally stopping it altogether?"

But that was yet to come. At this point the Beatles finished their world tour triumphantly, and approached America for their second visit—and first real tour—with absolute confidence.

San Francisco was the "kickoff" of a twenty-three-city tour. The New York Daily News of August 19, 1964, announced that they would make two stops in New York, one on August 28th and the other on September 20th.

The paper also noted that fewer than 10,000 Beatle fans turned out at the San Francisco airport—a Beatle letdown by the News' strange logic, for they easily estimated that at least 100,000 people should have been there.

This was the tail end of a long summer, and in the entire New York Times, on the day they arrived and the day after, there was no mention of the Beatles.

The four boys didn't care. They sang their way across America in the waning summer heat, from San Francisco to Las Vegas, up to Canada for a quick whistle stop in Vancouver, then to Seattle, Los Angeles, Denver, and Cincinnati.

That summer the Paramount Theater in Times Square announced that it would close for good and reviewers nostalgically recalled the "frenzied teenagers flocking there to swoon over Frankie Sinatra in the 1940s."

"It was only when big names played the Paramount that fans seemed to scream, the joint rock, and teenagers shriek in the aisles," Bosley Crowther recalled sadly in the Sunday Times. And another paper, with a sigh of relief announced that "Thank God those days of hysterical reaction are gone, gone, gone forever!"

That was the same day that Simon and Schuster began pushing die American edition of In His Own Write. The sixth printing, they said, brought the total sales up to 120,554 copies. In a country where literature is judged almost exclusively by sales, this was no small matter.

The Times said that the book had a touch of "inspired. nonsense" and Newsweek said it "frothed with original spontaneity," while Mademoiselle called it "marvelous" and even the Wall Street Journal admitted, "Mr. Lennon has written a zany and funny book."

The New York Public Library, however, in a poll of its readers, found less than one-tenth of one percent who had finished reading beyond page ten.

There was still no mention in the New York City papers of the Beatles, lost somewhere in the wilds of American touring. The big convention game in American politics had knocked them clear off the newspapers' front pages. Headlines screamed "Johnson Cool, Humphrey Hot" the very day the Beatles were due in New York City after eating up mileage in what was to end up as a 22,441-mile tour covering thirty performances.

The night of August 28th, the borough of Queens, in New York City, was put on the map of teenage America. It was there and then that the Beatles held a concert for a standing-room-only crowd of 16,000 in Forest Hills Stadium.

According to the Daily News the city was "Beatle Bombed." At least 2,500 girls staked out at Kennedy Airport as early as 3 A.M. when the boys' chartered plane flew in. A second wave of about the same number turned Park Avenue into an inferno m the area of the Delmonico Hotel, the pad the Beatles had picked for this visit.

The crowd remained at the hotel while 16,000 other children stormed into Forest Hills. The boys performed for only half an hour, and then took a helicopter back to the city and their hotel. They estimated a $40,000 take on the concert, which comes to more than a thousand dollars a minute. The girls, over 2,000 strong, had begun their vigil outside the Delmonico Hotel at dawn on August 28th, and they kept it up for the entire day, in spite of the fact that none of them caught sight of the boys in all that time. For all of their disappointment they didn't seem unhappy. It was almost as if it were enough to know they were near where the Beatles had to sleep.

The vigil drew one hundred policemen to keep order, along with twelve private guards assigned to block the hotel entrances.

A couple of times the girls rushed the guards at the hotel door, but were sent flying by mounted police. The girls, with banners and British flags chanted, "We want Ringo!" Ringo had somehow become the teenage sex symbol par excellence among four excellent sex symbols.

To encourage the crowd in the boys' absence, a number of disk jockeys in the hotel put on Beatle wigs and popped their heads out of the eighth-floor windows every few minutes, drawing piercing, hysterical shrieks from the girls. Actually, while they were in the hotel, the Beatles had a suite on the sixth floor.

The crowd outside the hotel was evidently not the crowd with tickets to the concert, for the police reported no diminution in the ranks that evening.

The Queens concert was a success, but, as was the way with Beatle concerts in general, no one knew what they sang.

"It was virtually impossible to hear the singing over the shrieking," Robert Shelton of the Times said. "The shrieking often reached the threshold of pain. It would be parlous to evaluate music-making in a situation like that. It sounded, to me, like a flock of transistor radios blaring in a bull ring.

"Their music finally stopped," he said, "but the malady lingered on."

The next day the papers reported a new outbreak of rioting in Philadelphia's Negro section, and this wiped all trace of the Beatles from their pages.

The Delmonico siege, however, continued for another day. The crowd of girls (no boys seemed allowed or involved) had dwindled to 1,000 on Park Avenue, but hundreds of others lurked in the side streets surrounding the Delmonico "plotting dark strategies to gain entrance to the hotel."

One girl tried to get in as Ringo's sister and had a small epileptic-type seizure when the police unmasked her. Three other girls took a cab to the front of the hotel and boldly announced that they lived in the penthouse.

"A good try," the police captain told them gently as he them packing.

Three others scaled the wall of a nearby building, scrambled to the roofs of others behind the hotel and worked their way up to the fourth-floor level and the hotel's water tower before they were caught.

Another group of twenty girls was trapped for thirty minutes in an elevator in an adjoining building as they tried an attempt to gain the roof.

Seemingly the most clever ruse, though it failed, was by three genuine Indians who arrived from the World's Fair in full regalia and claimed the Beatles had summoned them.

They were turned back to their hunting grounds in Flushing Meadow, but it turned out that they had been asked to come, legitimately, by a Beatle "aide" as an attempt to "amuse the boys."

This fooling around with peoples' time aroused one unfriendly policeman, who had been on duty close to the Beatles to label them a bunch of "choppers." "They think that they have enough money to tell the whole world to go to Hell—well, maybe they have."

So that the Beatles could leave the hotel the second night, a group of decoy men dashed out into waiting cars, amid screaming fans who converged from all points while the real Beatles sneaked out the side street and escaped in a car going the wrong way on a one-way street— with police escort.

After a twenty-five minute performance on the second night at Forest Hills Stadium, the boys returned to Manhattan by helicopter and took two limousines to Atlantic City.

From Atlantic City they went on to Philadelphia, Baltimore, Cleveland, New Orleans, Kansas City, Dallas, Memphis—to search out some Presley origins—and on September 20th, as the hot summer ebbed away and autumn came into New York City, the Beatles returned for a benefit performance at the dying Paramount.

There were "coolly elegant women in mink and pearls," according to Gay Talese of the Times, "rubbing shoulders with 3,600 teenagers."

There were also thousands of teenagers lining the streets around the theater with "Ringo for President!" signs. Remember, this was a presidential election year. But they also carried signs that read, "Beatles please stay here 4-ever."

"Anyone over twenty-one years of age," Talese said "felt ready for Social Security."

The concert this time lasted only twenty minutes. "Getting shorter each time they play," one bitter fan commented. They sang ten numbers—to the accompaniment of tossed jelly beans, slices of bread, and rolls of toilet paper—symbols all, whose inner meaning drew screams of recognition from the teenagers and bewildered head- shaking from the adults.

From the Paramount the boys were spirited away to the Riviera Idlewild Hotel overlooking the roaring traffic of the Van Wyck Expressway in Queens. Here they had a night of rest before they flew home.

"Only two people were in the lobby when the Beatles arrived," a newspaper reporter said. "They were both reading papers and went back to them when the Beatles disappeared up the elevators."

Bob Dylan, whom the Beatles had always admired, and who was to have a profound effect on their music, came to visit them that night, and the five sat up talking till early dawn.

The next day America shuddered a bit and shifted into its preelection fevers. Johnson stepped up the pace of his campaign and Goldwater accused him of avoiding issues, while Humphrey was labeled the least wealthy of the four main candidates.

And high over the Atlantic the four Beatles dozed their way back to England.

TOURING GREAT BRITAIN AND FILMING *HELP!*

WINTER, 1964, TO 1965

While the Beatles' American tours were filled with sound and fury, wild escapes from frantic teenage fans, and uneasy air flights across the continent, by contrast the British tours seemed filled with a pioneering element.

For one thing, the British tours took place in winter, the American tours in summer. In an account of the 1964 British tour, Neil Aspinall wrote, "Because of snow warnings, our driver, Alf, has got hold of chains for the Austin Princess plus an assortment of picks, shovels, and ropes.

Every time we go on the road I load up an electric kettle, a toaster, and a hair dryer."

The hair dryer is the most wonderful touch of all, but when you stop to think about it, the shaggy heads had to be just right for each performance and short of taking a hair-dresser along, a portable dryer was the only answer. According to Neil, they loaded their car and drove straight up England through the night, heading for Berwick-on-Tweed, a town less than a hundred miles from Glasgow. The boys resisted sleeping on these long rides, otherwise I they would arrive exhausted and only half-awake. "It's far better," George Harrison said, "to get a full night's sleep in a hotel than a miserable broken night's dozing on the road." But they were usually too tired, during these grueling rides, for any stimulating talk, and they'd make desultory conversation through the long, bleak hours while the car gunneled into the black night. The car radio would blast out talk and music to keep them awake till the last station went off the air, and then the absolute, utter boredom of the long ride would settle in.

An extra armchair was put in the back of the Princess, but it wasn't much of a success, although it was uncomfortable enough to keep anyone in it awake.

It's difficult to understand why the boys submitted to cramped and grueling rides unless you take into account the fact that they all four had a morbid fear of flying. They submitted to air travel in the American tour because trains were just too impractical, but they submitted to it unhappily with the firm conviction that they were eventually slated to die in a plane crash. When one of the planes they had chartered for an

American tour later crashed, they considered it not a matter of luck that they weren't aboard, but a sort of warning that their turn was still to come.

On this particular ride to Berwick-on-Tweed, they were in the last stages of mental exhaustion when a huge truck loomed up in the darkness behind them, started tailgating and flashing its lights.

Their car pulled to the side of the road and the truck driver leaned out of his cab and shouted, "Didn't you hear it fall off?"

"What!"

"One of them banjo things. It fell outta your car a couple of miles back."

Fearing it might be George's precious twelve-string guitar, they turned the car and moved back slowly, scanning each side of the road. After half an hour of painstaking search they found it, a battered and broken tangle of strings and wood.

"Well, at least it's not the twelve-string," George sighed in relief.

"Is it the bass?" Paul asked anxiously.

"It's George's spare Gretsch," Ringo decided after examining the wreckage in the car's headlights.

It wasn't a guitar George needed onstage, and philosophically the boys decided it could be worse. What was left could be cannibalized to repair other instruments. Yawning, they trudged back to the car, turned, and drove off into the long, dreary night.

On December 3rd they arrived in Glasgow after an icy drive from Berwick-on-Tweed. In the "civilization" of Glasgow the dreary monotony of the road vanished and the hysterical mania of the fans exploded around them.

"Tonight at the Odeon Theater," Neil wrote in a diary of the trip, "Beatle People, gave John, Paul, George, and Ringo a terrific welcome. I noticed that the strength of the security inside the theater had been tripled since our last visit. Everywhere you looked there were cops or attendants keeping the kids in their seats." The next day a heavy snow fell, and the boys started off before dawn for Newcastle. Getting them up to start early like that was a horrible task, according to Neil. "Like I most night people it takes them at least an hour to make friends with the world once they've opened their eyes," Neil said, and added that the worst way for them to start a day was to have to face a cheerful waiter with breakfast in their room. Neil, like a mother hen, would arrange for the trays to be left outside each door while he tiptoed about, waking each boy and allowing him to crawl out of bed and approach breakfast at his own speed.

Neil, who kept the same hours as the boys, saw nothing remarkable in his own role of combined nurse-mother. He accepted his sacrifices as part of the Beatle mystique. The Beatle breakfast consisted of orange juice, cereal, and boiled eggs. Paul sometimes favored fried eggs until, as he tells it, "John decided to join me and ordered a pair for himself. Lifting the lid from the dish he stared down at a ghastly fried embryo chick in one of the eggs."

After a long take John said, with a poker face, "It's not Easter or anything, is it then?"

From Newcastle, the boys cut across a 150-mile road E through the Pennines, a great chain of high, snowy mountains that run down the center of England. The road took them to Liverpool, a hard, dangerous ride on an icy, slippery surface. They made the city with no problems and in good time, but all keyed up with the tension of the drive.

In Liverpool a gaggle of relatives turned out for the performance, and so did Patti Boyd, who was staying with George's parents for the weekend.

Paul told of falling sucker to an age-old confidence trick at this show. He was making a phone call from a booth near the dressing room, and as he came out of the booth two teenage girls grabbed him.

"We've traveled five hundred miles to see tonight's concert," they told him, their lovely eyes sparkling with tears.

Remembering his own nightmarish ride over the hump of England, Paul said, "That's the greatest!" He smiled and tried to brush past into his dressing room.

"But we haven't got tickets! They're lost!"

"That's no good, is it?" He turned back and noticed their tears again. "Well, it's hard for me to get you in, but I'll tell you what. I'll tell the man at the door that you're relatives of mine, and he'll have to let you through."

Captivated by his own generosity, and carried away by the role he took them into the dressing room and introduced them around as long-lost cousins. Then he arranged to have them stand in the wings and watch. It was a magnanimous gesture, soured just a little by his eventual discovery that the two girls lived only a few blocks away in downtown Liverpool.

Including the Liverpool concert, this British tour took in eighteen different towns in England, Scotland, and Wales with each concert a complete sellout.

The tour had arranged one free day after the Liverpool concert to let the boys visit with their families. Med, detailing that day, tells how George spent it with his folks and Patti Boyd, the girl he was to marry. Ringo spent it with his folks in Liverpool's suburbs. John's Aunt Mum had moved to a seaside resort, so John and Paul visited the McCartneys, Paul's father and his new wife.

"They got up very early," Neil recalls, "at around ten o'clock—well, early for them—and Paul fetched his two moped bikes [Bikes with small motors fitted to them.]

"I don't think it's a good idea to go out bike that Paul's father warned them. "You'll be recognized right away."

"Not in the get-up I've planned," Paul reassured him and put on a shabby raincoat, a beret with his hair pulled under it, and a false mustache. To complete the picture he borrowed a pair of his father's glasses.

The idea seemed fine till they ran out of gas and stopped at a service station with an attendant. While John turned his face away, Paul said, "Fill 'er up, please!" in his best American accent. The attendant grinned. "Sure, Paul, but why the funny clothes?"

Pulling off his hat in chagrin, Paul asked, "How did you recognize me?"

"I'd know that voice anywhere, luv. It's blasting out of every record store in town," she told him cheerfully as she filled the tank.

It's hard to know if the whole stunt wasn't an attempt to bring out a bit more attention on the off chance that they wouldn't, be recognized without a disguise. But without the elaborate getup they were spotted again that afternoon. They had borrowed a car to' cruise around the outskirts of Liverpool, and they stopped at an antique shop to browse. Before ibey had dosed the door behind them, the street outside was jammed with jams, girls and boys. Eventually the police had to be called to get them to the safety of their car.

After Liverpool they went on to Manchester, which they reached at rush hour. Here the ear was stuck for five hours in a thick, yellow industrial fog, Manchester's contribution to air pollution. As a result, they were fifteen minutes late for the concert, a live television broadcast.

By the time they went onstage, the studio was rocking with disappointed fans screaming, "We want the Beatles."

There is no indication of the reaction of the home audience.

The fog kept them stranded in Manchester, and they booked into the Midland; a big luxury hotel. An impromptu press conference was arranged, and also an interview with a little American girl reporter who had flown in from Hartford, Connecticut, to interview them.

As luck would have it, Walter Shenson, the producer of *A Hard Day's Night*, was in town. He dropped in and they talked till three in the morning, making plans for their new movie, at that time tentatively based on a story called A Talent for Loving. That might they decided not to use the story and in a negative mood, probably engendered by the miserable fog, they also decided not to play themselves in this new picture, whatever the script might be.

The next day they fled Manchester to a quiet country club in Spinkhill outside of Sheffield. Another group of singers, the Moody Blues, were at the same club, and that night the two groups organized a wild billiard game which lasted till two in the morning.

Since none of the four Beatles had ever learned to shoot billiards they discarded all traditional rules and invented a new game, which started with a white billiard ball in the center of the table. Using the flat, handle ends of the cues, they belted the ball up and down the table as fast as they could. Each team defended one end of the table: the object of the game was to shoot the ball past the opposing team against the table edge.

The ball hurtled back and forth, up and down the table wildly all eight players hilariously slamming it back and forth as hard as they could with no regard for damage to able. New rules governing the play were put into action as fast as they could be dreamed up.

Commenting on the game, Lennon said, "This is gear. We must always stay in country clubs, Neil. You just can't do this sort of thing in hotels."

The brief expedition to a reluctantly lost childhood cheered all of them, and continued to warm them on the wet, cold ride from Sheffield to Birmingham. As the ride ended, and they came into Birmingham, the familiar nightmare took over.

The Birmingham police had set up a special plan to have the boys meet a pair of escorting vehicles outside the city.

From then on it was more of the old familiar panic, shrieking and desperate racing from waiting cars to dressing rooms and then back to the cars.

From Birmingham they headed for London and an extra day to allow John and Ringo to visit their wives after an absence of ten days. After that the tour was wound up.

"I suppose the most fantastic shows of all came toward of the series," Neil said, "when we went to London to play at two of the largest movie houses in Britain, the Hammersmith Odeon and the Finsbury Park Astoria."

Hammersmith was just about the wildest of the lot. Nearly 3,500 fans packed the theater. As soon as the Beatles went onstage the entire audience stood up. Spectators began climbing on each others' shoulders and surging toward the stage ominously.

Thirty London bobbies linked arms all the way across the front of the auditorium in a desperate attempt to keep the frantic girls from storming the stage.

They played an insane concert with the deafening noise of screaming girls drowning out any attempt at music. This was one of the concerts where the term "jet scream" was coined to describe the physically painful result of all those shrieking girls.

In terms of their reception in any big city such as London, the Beatles could easily compare the British tours to the American. It was the other, quiet times, the long, dreary drives through winter nights, the deserted country clubs, the absolute loneliness of vast stretches of country, that made the British tours so different.

That February, right after the British tour, the filming of their second movie *Help!* was started. The location chosen for the climax of the film was Nassau, in the British Bahamas. The arrival of the boys in Nassau was described by reporter Alan Levy, new to the Beatle-watching game.

"Beatlemania no longer happens," Levy said wonderingly. "It is made!"

Admitting he didn't know how it had worked in their early days, at this point he decided it was the result "Not so much of deliberate staging as of ineptitude. It is a product of what psychiatry calls the self-fulfilled prophecy."

In other words, if you accept the fact that a thing is inevitable then it is bound to happen. By this rule, one way to incite a Beatle riot is to expect one and attempt to create an antiriot atmosphere.

When he arrived in Nassau a few days ahead of the Beatles, Levy felt that a full-fledged riot was in the making. He mentioned a "mystery man" who had appeared on the island a few months earlier and, with a flock of accompanying rumors, had started buying up land to conceal the Beatles when they arrived.

This secrecy was the best way to attract attention, and when the Beatles' agent finally arrived and asked for a briefing with Nassau officials, a week before the boys arrived, it attracted even more attention. To avert disaster when the Beatles flew in, the aide suggested that they be spirited away from the field to a secret press conference.

No official of Nassau expected any assault on the boys. But they had read about other demonstrations, so they all got together and hatched out a plan of "protective deception."

About two hundred fans turned out for the arrival of the Beatles, an orderly gathering, mostly young girls from eight to sixteen. A dozen policemen were scattered around the airport, but everyone felt there was little to fear. The fans had come to look, not touch—but all this was before the "protective deception" was started.

By evening, the Beatle plane touched down at a distant runway and under cover of darkness, concealed from the fans, the Beatles disembarked and drove off in a limousine. Then the plane taxied properly to a landing gate.

The crowd cheered as four young men in Beatle cuts came out of the plane. Amid the cheering, banners were unfurled reading, WE LOVE YOU BEATLES. Everybody pressed up for an orderly look at the boys and discovered to their chagrin that the four men were ringers wearing wigs, not the Beatles at all.

The crowd's cheerful attitude of welcome changed to fury when they realized that they had been tricked. They rushed to the parking lot and tumbled into their cars and gave chase to the escaping limousine.

Motorcycles and cars tore after it with their horns blasting.

"Cars veered from one side of the road to the other, Levy reported. "Motorcycles out in front of autos. Three cars traveling abreast rounded a two-lane curve."

By some miracle there was no accident, but the next day the newspaper headlines screamed, "Beatles Lead Terror Drive."

The Beatles scurried into the concert hall for the press conference, which, according to Levy, was grotesque. The boys looked fatigued and bored. Ringo and Paul sipped Scotch, George had a Coke, and John water. A radio man pushed a mike in front of George and asked with unusual wit. "Written any good books lately, John?"

John was then asked, "How many songs have you written, Paul?" '

Confused, a lady challenged Paul. "Young man, which one are you?"

"Me? I'm Roger," Paul snapped. "Now don't forget it."

Outside, during the press conference, the mob that had chased them from the airport waited, howling and furious at having been cheated. Had they not been cheated, Levy is positive they would have welcomed them calmly 'at the airport with a few shouts and calls. Instead, a real air of Beatlemania had been created.

After the conference the deception was continued the boys whisked out a back entrance, while the police reassured the waiting crowd, which had started to calm down, "They'll be right out. They'll be coming this way." When they had been gone for five minutes, the police inspector opened the door and announced triumphantly and hopefully, "They've already gone. You might as well all go back home."

The crowd, angry and cheated, surged forward and broke into the empty conference hall to tear it apart snatching at glasses and ashtrays as souvenirs.

Things settled down a bit in the days that followed and shooting on the film started. The script had a tropical sequence, and even in February Nassau was sunny and bright enough.

The plot, kept secret by Walter Shenson for some obscure reason—perhaps fear that it would frighten the fans away—was leaked to the press "inadvertently" by Ringo Starr.

"There's this cult that's after me from somewhere in the far east. One of the members of the cult is a fan of mine and she sent me a magic ring from their temple and now they're all after me to get it back.

"I get the ring on my finger, but I can't get it off until the movie's end when they get it back, otherwise they'd have to kill me to get it, and Mr.. Shenson says that'd disturb our fans too much, to say nothing of me."

The earlier film, A Hard Day's Night, had brought out Ringo's remarkable flair for pathos. Capitalizing on it, Shenson cast him in the lead in Help!

As for the exotic plot and locale, Shenson said, "We don't want the Beatles' second movie to be like their first one. [It wasn't!] What we're trying to do is give it all the effect of a comic strip. The picture is completely wild, mad, way, way out."

Richard Lester, the director, one who had so successfully done the first film, summed up their aims in *Help!* "We're trying to make the movie surrealistic with sudden cuts and unexpected happenings.

"Ringo may be fighting with a tiger in one scene, doing something completely different in the next. We want to keep the audience off balance, in a state where they cannot anticipate what will happen next. The costumes are as extravagant as they would be in a comic strip.

"We're aiming," he elaborated, "at a correlation between pop music and pop art by producing a pop movie."

Unfortunately this aim was lost somewhere in the shooting and they may not have made a conventional movie, but at the same time they didn't make a pop movie.

Labeling it a transitional movie, Lester told the press that the boys were still playing themselves, in spite of an earlier decision to become more versatile.

"By the next movie they can go on and develop into characters like W. C. Fields."

Fields, however, by all accounts merely played himself, and it's noteworthy that while Lennon had the courage to play another character in *How I Won The War*, the others decided to give up movies after *Help!*, declaring that they hated the "whole bit." Such declarations should be accepted cautiously, because Ringo is currently playing a role in the moving picture version of Candy.

In Nassau, during the filming of *Help!* Ringo insisted he loved film making and John was enraptured by the special brand of magic cinematography evokes. "I like making movies," he said at the time, a statement he contradicted vehemently later on. "I'd make as many movies as they'd want me to. I like to see the rushes so I can tell what or what not to do next time. When I first saw scenes from *A Hard Day's Night* I could see how nervous I looked.

Something in my face was twitching. Later on, although I still felt nervous, I was able to control the twitch.

"Most of all," he finally admitted, "I enjoy making records. Why? Well, it's something you can follow right through from writing the song to the recording session. It gives you a complete feeling."

George Harrison, too, put in his vote for movie making. "I get such a wonderful feeling of satisfaction out of making a film. When you're through with all the time spent and the standing around and everything, at least you've got something. I want to get a 16mm print of A Hard Day's Night, and one of this picture too, and of any others we make. That way, when I'm about ninety years old I can pull them out and show them and prove to my great-great-grandchildren that I really did something, really made something."

In a more speculative mood, George added, "Music is fine, but I enjoy making people laugh. If they can laugh at us in the movies, that's wonderful. Even if they laugh at our music, well, we've made somebody happy, and I like that.

"Most of our fans range from thirteen to seventeen and I'm curious to see what happens as they grow older, whether they stick with us or drop off." [What George didn't foresee was that the Beatles themselves would grow older and change, along with their fans.]

"Since we made the movie, A Hard Day's Night, a lot of middle-aged people have come to like us too, even though they may not like our music so much. It's a funny thing about older people liking us. Six months ago some of the really 'in' teenagers in England switched from us to the Rolling Stones because they felt that we were gettin" to be accepted by middle-aged people, by the Establishment, and they wanted no part of that. You know, their rebellion has a certain conformity. It has to conform to what the Establishment doesn't like!"

"None of us is really a good musician," Paul said commenting on their ability and how the fans view them.

"We don't know how to read or write music. We're just natural musicians."

Asked if their music was good, Paul countered with, "Since we're naturals, we're really not qualified to call something good or bad. We just know what we like. If we write something and we like it, well, that's the main thing.

"Look, I don't believe in criticism. No one wants to hear someone else tell them that they've done something bad. Even constructive criticism doesn't work out. It puts you down instead of encouraging you."

After a moment's thought, he amended that. "Of course with us it's different. When we criticize each other, I mean, we're so close it's like criticizing ourselves. Self-criticism can help. Like John and I both sign all our songs, but sometimes I compose one and John composes. Once I wrote a line, 'Well, she was just seventeen,' I looked for a line to rhyme and came up with one that didn't even scan, 'She had never been a beauty queen.'

"John straightened me out and changed the second line to, 'You know what I mean.' Actually it doesn't mean anything, but it sounds deep."

Speculating on their meaning, a task they usually leave to others, Paul McCartney said, "We were just a joke before A Hard Day's Night. People, adults, that is, didn't take us seriously. We were just something their kids wanted to listen to. Then, when their kids dragged them to the movies, they saw for themselves and seemed to like us,"

Help!, when it was finally released, bore little resemblance to A Hard Day's Night. It had none of the art technique of the first film, but it did have a wild, far-out quality that has been copied over and over.

The technique that Lester referred to as "comic book style" has been used to death on television, particularly in series called "The Monkees" and in almost every sequence that shows a pop music group.

When Help! was released, the technique was still new and exciting, but without writer Alun Owen, who did the first movie, Lester and Shenson seemed unable to achieve the New Wave quality of A Hard Day's Night. Help! was slicker and more polished cinematographically, and its use of color was exciting, but as a picture it was much emptier.

The boys acted not at all. What there was of excitement was achieved with sound and color and clever editing. The few mumbled speeches given to the Beatles were delivered flatly and tonelessly, deliberately so, apparently. None of the boys lost his cool, even when threatened with disembowelment or manhandling by a tiger.

Ringo, when it was suggested that his finger be cut off to get rid of the sacrificial ring, looked at the camera with an expressionless face and said, "But I'm used to that finger, y'know."

John, Paul, and George were so slightly characterized in the movie that in the course of it one could easily forget which was which. The glimpse of characterization in *A Hard Day's Night* was never realized in *Help!* The boys were a million miles away from the audience, far more lively removed than any actor m any Hollywood picture. The noise level was lower than it was in *A Hard Day's Night,* and the music better, in fact the most enjoyable part of the film was the music.

It seems odd that no attempt was made to get any acting out of the four. Action, yes. They run and swing and chase madly around, but there is not one whisper of acting.

The reviewers, when *Help!* was released in America some six months later, seemed a bit bewildered by it Bosley Crowther of the New York Times said the kindest way to describe it is to label it ninety minutes of good clean insanity.

Speaking of clean insanity, the only moment in the film that could, by the wildest imagination be called remotely salacious, is when Paul, in place of a guitar, strums at a girl m a bikini, but in a hilarious rather than off-color way.

"There's nothing in *Help!*" Crowther said, "to compare with that wild ballet of the Beatles racing across a playground in *A Hard Day's Night,* nothing as wistful as the ramble of Ringo around London all alone. Those were the episodes that gave a welcome respite to the frantic pace and mood of that film. This one, without sense or pattern, is wham, wham, wham all the way."

On the other hand, Judith Crist of the New York Herald Tribune said she liked *Help!* even better than *A Hard Day's Night.* She conceded, right off the bat, that "it lacks the initial impact and delighted surprise of that first encounter with the Beatles." She calls Lester a bit self-indulgent and points to traces of "infatuation with sight of one's own gags," but goes on to say the movie more than compensates for any lack of freshness by "providing the nonacting Beatles at their most relaxed.

"There's a glorious madness to the masquerades, traps, horrible machines and horribler machinations," Crist concludes. "Charm is the word, and the wonder of *Help!* is that without a leer or a lapse of taste it

112

provides fun all the way."

In the New York World Telegram and Sun, Leonard Harris found it genuinely funny, smartly written and directed, but noted that it had its weaknesses. "It gets mechanical towards the end and drags."

Archer Winsten, in the Post, noted the calm, don't-give-a-damn element of the Beatles. "Like so many pictures of the more esoteric sort coming from Italy or France," Winsten said in an analytic mood, "the film tries to be more than it says, and this gives the deeper thinkers a chance to inject then: own favorite interpretations of this or that unobvious maneuver." In the end, however, he sums up the picture as "halfway between hysteria and incoherence, occasionally tied to something recognizable as satire."

WHAT ARE THE BEATLES REALLY LIKE?

A RESPITE IN TIME

The question constantly asked about any person in the public eye is, "What is he really like?"

After reading about where the Beatles have been and what they've done, after finding out that they've become a legend in five or six years and musically have spoken with rare eloquence to a sizable part of our population, the question still remains, "What are they really like?"

This is a hard enough question to answer when it is asked about anyone we know well, our child, our mate, our parents, our friends—even ourselves.

How much harder it is to answer when the person we ask about is constantly in the public eye. A part of the shield he raises to defend himself against the public is his personality. What really exists behind that personality may be jealously treasured in a desperate hope for privacy.

Charles Chaplin has come alive for us on the screen and generation after generation felt their hearts go out to the foolish, wistful tramp. We know, however, that Chaplin himself is neither foolish nor wistful. The tramp is a personality created by the man.

With every entertainer, the projected personality is a creation of either the man himself or his public-relations staff. Marlene Dietrich has become a sex symbol for the ages, but every indication is that she was and is a warm hausfrau under the symbol, although there is even some indication that the hausfrau is simply another "created" personality to hide the real woman. Marilyn Monroe, another sex symbol, seems to have been a lonely, frightened, and not-too-clever girl. Grade Alien, the epitome of mental fluff, was a bright, shrewd woman

Even apart from the world of entertainment, we all accept the fact that a politician's image has no connection with the reality of the man.

How then with the Beatles? Are they geniuses or idiots, muddle-headed, or shrewd business men, lovable mop heads or polished juvenile delinquents?

Some hint of the truth may be in their own words. "The thing that bothers me," Paul McCartney once said, "is our image, the image the public has of us. When it's reported that we drink or smoke, they're upset. But we're the same as everybody else. Most young people our age drink and smoke.

George Harrison disagreed somewhat. "I think most people are beginning to accept us now for what we are. Our image is changing."

John Lennon said, "Don't get the idea that we sit around thinking of our public image or anything. Were just ourselves, that's all."

But what is "just ourselves"?

George Harrison tried to define their reaction to life in terms of success and financial security. "As success comes, life gets easier in a way, but the pressure gets worse the pressure to make each record, each movie better than the one before. It's like the show business gag, what will you do for an encore? Each time you've got to top yourself, and everyone is sitting around waiting to see if you can do it—maybe hoping that you can't.

"One thing we're all agreed on is that we like money. I've never heard of anyone who didn't, actually. People m the United States all think we're from the slums. Well our families have always worked. There's always been steady pay coming in. Before we had all this money, sure, we said, I'll buy this, I'll buy that-but when you get the money you're in a big rush to buy anything. You ask yourself if you really want it first"

Paul McCartney agreed with this and added, I like money for the things you can get with it, but I also like the idea that I've got the money. Everyone says money can't buy you health or it can't buy you happiness, but we all know that.

"When we were just beginning to be successful we were in a panic for fear it would all stop before we had a chance to make enough to keep us later on. Now we have it and we like it fine."

John Lennon seconded this. "I could even retire now. I've got enough money. But retire? What would I do? Nothing?"

Their need for security along with their disinterest, real or affected, in material things, has been stressed by all of them, and they all feel it in the same way. Their attitudes toward security and wealth, like most of their other attitudes, are similar. It's part of the Beatle mystique, this solidity of opinion, this closeness and togetherness.

All of them feel it and it's a closeness that's more like marriage than friendship. "I live in a home that's twenty-eight miles from London," George once said, and John quickly added, "I've moved to a house outside

115

of London too."

"We've known each other for such a long time," George then said thoughtfully, attempting a definition if not an explanation of the Beatle mystique.

"We spend most of our time together, even when we're working. If a couple of us go out separately, we'll probably end up in the same place before the night's over.

"I went to school with Paul. I've known him about nine years now, and John for seven. I've known Ringo four years."

Nodding, Ringo said, "But even four years have had an effect. When I'm alone I look around and feel that something's missing without the other three."

It is, in show business, something of a rarity for a team to get along this well, to feel this much harmony and rapport, and the harmony evidently extends to the wives of the married Beatles as well. The Stair, Lennon, and Harrison ladies allow no hint of discord to mar the image of togetherness.

As a group the Beatles function well and present a single image to the world. Reporters have described them as "a delightful foursome," "decent, witty and sensible."

However, not everyone has been charmed with the boys. Writer Alan Levy, interviewing them in Nassau during the filming of *Help!*, noted that John Lennon spoke with a kind of surly finality. "Mostly he just heckled the others. Nothing he said was especially witty or important, but he spoke every line as if it were the perfect squelch."

Levy either exaggerated John's unpleasantness, or else irritated him for some reason. Whatever happened, there appears to have been little rapport. He asked George Harrison about Beatlemania and received a sharp answer. "You're a bit behind the times, aren't you? A year or two ago it was Beatlemania. Now it's just fan worship."

"Beatlemania isn't difficult to define," Paul explained. "It's Rudolph Valentino-mania, only younger."

Ringo told Levy, "The only thing fan worship tells me is my bank balance. As long as it all goes on I don't have to look at my bank book."

"Would you miss it, if it stopped?" Levy asked.

"Not really," Ringo said. "We all know it can't go on forever and we'll have some notice before it plays out, some warning. It'll never stop in just one day "

"I wouldn't be sick if it did," John put in. "I can adapt to anything."

Paul, toward the end of the interview, said, "You haven't asked us a single question that we haven't been yet." Levy wondered, "here was the man who had been asked everything! All I could say was, "Can you think of any question you've never been asked?"

He shook his head, and Ringo said sadly, "Not even that." Levy reflected, "I scarcely envied these four, good-natured, rather touching millionaires, cooped up in their prison of super-success. They had proved to be neither the long-haired wits that some adult intellectuals take them for, nor the guttersnipes that a Nassau hostess labeled them when they serenaded her with a ditty that began, 'She's a fat old bag.'

Keith Althan, a feature writer for a teenage magazine, noted back in 1966 that Lennon was often called sarcastic and cynical. It was said that he didn't care about anything.

"If that is true of Lennon now," Althan said, "it was also true of him three years ago, and it's probably because he was the most well-defined character in the group before they came to fame, and the most mature."

Lennon, Althan suggested, had changed the least of all the Beatles. "Fame stamped nothing on John Lennon. John Lennon stamped on fame.

"The achievement of having written two books means far more than all the money he has earned," Althan went on, and he quoted Lennon as saying, " 'It proved to people that I could do something else and it proved it to me, which was more important.'"

Another glimpse of Lennon's character comes from Neil Aspinall, who is absolutely partial to the Beatles. Neil told of a "humorous" incident that doesn't shed a very good light on John.

The boys had gone into a posh tea shop for the traditional afternoon tea and cake. Paul said to John in what Neil described as a classy accent, "You are going to be the mother then, luv?"

"I am that," John answered in a thick Lancastershire drawl. He then picked up the large teapot and went all around the table pouring from cup to cup. "The thing was," Neil said, "he didn't lift the pot between each cup, so in addition to filling the cups he also saturated the tablecloth.

"The waitress had a hard time of it trying to ignore us barbarians," Neil went on in delight at what he considered a "fun" stunt.

"John was getting the greatest kick out of it all. The topper was the way he tipped. He left the money in a teacup, and the cup was full of tea."

It's a nasty, unpleasant little incident, and one that hardly improves John's image.

Another picture of John was given by Larry Kane, now in the news department at radio station WFIL in Philadelphia. Kane traveled with the Beatles in 1964 on their tour across America and went with them again in 1965. He became very close to the boys, as close perhaps as any newsman could get.

During his first trip with the Beatles, Kane tells of the contrast between his own business suit and tie and the Beatles' casual jeans and T-shirts. At one point Lennon, who had been standoffish, considered Kane's clothes and said, "You're kind of square, aren't you?"

"It's better than looking like a slob!" Kane snapped back. Instead of alienating Lennon, it won him over, and from then on Kane was accepted by John, and, through him, by the others.

Summing up the Beatles' attitude to their own success, Kane said, "To this day I'm sure that they know what they were before it all started.

"Lennon is the quickest-witted man I've ever met, and the sharpest, but I think he had all this before he became a Beatle."

"He put down reporters often, and the reason they did such 'jobs' on him was that they couldn't understand what he was doing, the distaste he felt .at their questions. Not that he wouldn't go along with any decent interview, but, for example, the sample questions at press conferences that first year were, 'What do you use on your corn flakes?' 'Do you like steak rare, medium, or well-done?' Can you blame them for getting sick and tired of such questions? They told me 'We're human beings more than anything else.'"

This is what they were trying so desperately to establish in those early years, that they were human beings doing human things and feeling human emotions. They were not animals and not Beatles.

In an attempt to define this feeling, Lennon has said he felt no different now that he was rich. He just felt more secure and that was all he ever wanted to feel, security.

The boys never had money in their pockets on these tours. Epstein used to give them an allowance of $15U a week as spending money, and the rest he would invest for them. When anyone asked them about money or holdings, they would just shrug and say, "We leave all that to

Brian."

Lennon doesn't have much fondness for Americans in spite of all the money he has collected here. He has some deep convictions about the immorality of the Vietnam War, and he has viewed President Johnson as "a hypocrite."

Of the four, Kane believes that Lennon is the most religious. He has discussed religion quite a lot in a searching and inquiring, if by no means orthodox, way.

None of the boys is an atheist. Ringo claims to be an agnostic and so does Paul, but they believe in something, according to Kane, something they just cannot define.

At press conferences they have always tried to be honest when people asked them questions. That's something reporters have ripped Lennon, in particular, apart for. Lennon is honest. And fortunately or unfortunately, he is in a position few people hold. He used to say, "We're on a platform. Why not use it for saying what we believe?"

"Don't you think it could be used improperly?" he asked,

"Sure, but I don't think we ever would."

Looking back at all the things they have said and done, it's rather easy to believe Lennon's sincerity and good sense. His reputation for sarcasm and cynicism is probably the inevitable result of an honest man fed up to the gills with the machinations of creating news stories.

Unlike John Lennon, Paul McCartney is the "charmer of the Beatles." He hides a sharp intellect behind a facade of schoolboy enthusiasm, because he has realized that people are more at home with the boy than with the man. Of all the Beatles, Paul has been the most responsible for seeing to it that the image of the group has remained one of cooperation with the press and the public. He has often, annoyed at his own instinct to please, tried unsuccessfully to become less cooperative, more ruthless.

Of his own success, Paul once said, "We haven't changed as people. Circumstances have changed. You don't turn into a monster overnight because you're making a lot of money. The remote idol was an image we shattered," he insisted. "We're people first and last."

In spite of this pronouncement, Larry Kane believes that Paul has been changed by success the most of the four. "I like him best, but he's the one most affected by all o Paul according to Kane, has always been the glamor of the group and he has played the role to the hilt, enjoying every moment of it. He likes putting people on, but in a good-natured way, always mindful of his image.

"Paul was always combing his hair," Kane said, always looking in a mirror, very self-conscious about his appearance. He took great pains with his clothes. When we were on a plane during the tours, Paul would go into the John and comb his hair and prepare himself for his fans before he got off. The other three couldn't care less how they looked."

Paul himself has often stressed the independence ha success has brought. "I don't have to answer to a boss, he said. "Most people want to tell the man in charge that they are going to do things their way. That's what we do now, and I like that, though in a sense I guess we've always done it."

According to Paul the driving force in his life is composing. "Song writing is something I can't stop. I could never sit back and do nothing. Even if the four of us eventually break up I'll want to go on writing songs."

George Harrison, the quiet Beatle, is the most mature of the four. "When we didn't have much money," he has said "there didn't seem to be a lot of things we wanted. Now that we have money, I still can't think of many things I want. Oh, I'd like a motorboat, but certainly not a yacht or an airplane, and yet both are easily available."

"I think if I hadn't become successful with the group, I'd still be doing the same thing somewhere else—probably less successfully."

George once said, rather wistfully, "We don't want to be always setting examples to people. We enjoy the music we play and the films we make, but we don't want to put ourselves on a pedestal and say we're gods now. We just want to be normal and stay sane and have a great time. Is that asking so much?"

Larry Kane has claimed George Harrison is a very unusual case. "He's the only one I thought out of place with the others. He was the quietest and kept to himself. In fact he was the only one who honestly didn't like the publicity, who didn't like the lights.

"If you ever watch him onstage, he's turned inward, involved in his own music, concentrating on sound. Off-stage he's hard to know, curt and short, though perhaps that's simply an extension of his shyness."

George had a thing about American comic books. He couldn't get enough of them, and he read them constantly.

The other three teased him about this all during the tours, and in fact it was used as a sight gag in *Help!* where George sat at a piano whose music rack held a row of comic books. None of the Beatles has ever read much, at least while on tour, when their only real relaxation was playing Monopoly and poker. They really became tremendously I caught up in Monopoly, and personally considered it the biggest feature of their American tours. George was the most ardent Monopoly player of the four. Larry Kane sees Ringo Starr as the most sincere of the Beatles, at least sincere in the sense that he has always been the plainest, the least pretentious. His almost grateful attitude toward the fans is real, Kane insists. He is the waving type. He'll wave from planes, buses, limousines, from anywhere. He has always looked out at the world with a glum face, but it is Ringo's face. It's the way he looks, and the glumness is only on the outside. In reality he is a voluble man, a man who talks a lot. Ringo is also probably the most domestic. His feelings about home, about marriage and children are probably more extensive than the others'. Perhaps it's because his background was poorer. Whatever it is, he talks more of his own family and his father and mother than the others do.

During the 1965 tour, Kane asked him, "Ringo, if you had a fourteen-year-old kid who went out to the Hollywood Bowl and acted the way the Hollywood teenagers acted during a Beatle concert, would you get upset?"

He shrugged and said, "If I had a kid that age I damned well wouldn't let her go to a Beatle concert!"

"I also asked Ringo what his ambition was," Kane recalled, "and he answered that his total ambition, his final one, was to set up a chain of hairdressing salons. You know, his wife was a hairdresser when he met her."

In spite of the fact that the Beatles are not intellectuals, Kane stressed the fact that they have always had rather firm opinions about everything.

Politically, they were definitely against conservatism m England. At first, during the 1964 tour of America, they were very pro-Labour. Later, disillusionment set in, or else their financial position changed their viewpoint. They talked a lot about the British tax situation, but their attitude seemed to be that they were helping their country by the money they earned and the taxes they paid.

They respect royalty, but it is a token respect and not too deep. Kane found them socialistic, with views a lot more liberal than those of most Americans. Internationally they had none of the distrust of Communist countries held by Kane and the other American members of the entourage.

"What impressed them most about America, Kane said, "was the Western way of life. When they came here in 1964 they only wanted to buy records of country and Western singers like Hank Snow and Eddie Arnold. They were in love with the Nashville Sound, and they hoped to find the roots of it. They wanted to go to Nashville, but they never made it."

Ringo particularly began to plunge into the whole Western bit. He bought an endless supply of boots and

Western shirts, Western ties, pants, outlandish and garish souvenirs. Cities like Chicago and New York Just weren't the real America to them.

What struck Kane about the four Beatles was their decency. "They were gentlemen. They addressed older men as sir, and rarely cursed in public. Sure, part of it was put on, but a big part of it was real." They had a tremendous natural humor, Kane recalls, especially in press conferences. Indeed, press conferences were a show in themselves. Reporters would ask a simple question and get a funny answer, or a funny-sarcastic answer. One reporter on the first and second tour always I used to ask, "What are you going to do when the bubble bursts?"

Finally, in disgust, Lennon snapped, "I'm going to sit back and count my money." By 1965 they knew what they would do—they knew that they would expand. McCartney once said, "It's obvious that I'm not going to have long hair when I'm fifty. I think what we'll all do is continue to use our combined talents to produce something new, maybe a new sound in music."

Now Paul's prophecy has come true. They've left their old Beatle ways behind and have done albums which have become legendary in their own time. They have always had a deep sense of obligation to the fans who made them. As evidence of this sense of obligation, when promoters. In some cities charged seven dollars for tickets based on what the traffic would bear, the Beatles became very upset and fought bitterly to prevent it.

Eventually they managed a clause in most of their contracts that set a ceiling on the price of tickets.

Their protective attitude toward their fans and their fear of exploitation has often carried them to strange lengths. In the Edgewater Hotel in Seattle during the 1964 tour, they found out that the maids had planned to cut their bedsheets up and sell the pieces as souvenirs. The boys felt this was outright exploitation, but whether of themselves or the buyers isn't clear.

To frustrate the attempt they poured milk, liquor, and orange juice all over the sheets and made it impossible to salvage them. It was a strange way of handling the situation and hardly speaks for their maturity, but it may have sprung from their innate honesty. The total picture of the Beatles presents them as essentially level-headed, normal young men. They drank a great deal during their tours, but not excessively. They drank out of boredom, the way any young men will. If they could be criticized about anything in the way of drinking, it would be for mixing Scotch with Coke, their favorite drink, something to make an American shudder.

The opportunity to have just about any young woman they wanted was always present, but all the men who traveled with them on their tours stressed the fact that they never took advantage of these opportunities. They were normal, healthy young men and they acted as normal men always have, but there were no wild parties, no sex orgies as the newspapers constantly hinted. They seem to have behaved with admirable balance and restraint, and with an eye constantly on their public image.

THEY RECEIVE THE ORDER OF THE BRITISH EMPIRE AND MEET ELVIS PRESLEY

JUNE TO AUGUST, 1965

On the night of June 11, 1965, the Beatles crossed a decisive social barrier. They were included by Queen Elizabeth in her birthday honors list and named Members of the Most Excellent Order of the British Empire (MBE).

Although in the past, actors, dancers, and singers had been named for membership, the Beatles were the first group of pop singers to make the list.

The Order of the British Empire is a historically recent list, started in 1917 by King George V, and there are five classes to it. The highest is Knight, Grand Cross and the lowest is Member (MBE).

The honor, while it delighted the boys, met with mixed reactions in Great Britain. The teenage view was, "Well, that's done it. They've become respectable, and we want nothing to do with them."

The older, respected Establishment members in Britain looked at the whole thing askance. It was another example of decaying standards.

After the presentation the boys posed for endless photographs, wisecracked at press conferences, and carefully stowed away the honorary silver badges and pink ribbons while they turned their attention to their coming tour of America, their third visit and their second tour.

This 1965 tour, starting August 15th and ending August 31st, was slated to include ten cities only, and it was taken at the height of their career. They were as popular as they had ever been. Epstein, who had managed their first tour very carefully, making sure that they never had to play in stadiums with empty seats, had no such worry this time. Their very first concert, given in New York City, filled Shea Stadium, a colossal bowl that accommodates 55,600 fans. At $5.65 per ticket, it was a complete sellout long in advance. Blocks of tickets were bought up by various groups, some charitable and some that benefited only themselves, and then "scalped" for up to $100.00 a seat.

Sid Bernstein, a New York entrepreneur who promoted the show, boasted at the time that he could fill Shea Stadium again, if only the Beatles would hang around the city long enough to do two shows.

New York City viewed the entire proceedings with an awed sense of deja vu. All of this had happened before, hadn't it? Even the Beatles' takeoff from London Airport had a familiar ring. Four hundred screaming teenagers watched policemen brawl with photographers and newsmen while the Beatles posed and smiled and waved.

The brawl started when a plains-clothes police superintendent tried to push the photographers back and a uniformed police sergeant and constable charged the newsmen and scattered them. Not knowing who the plainclothesman was, the photographers fought back, and a battle got under way at the same time as the jet plane.

While they sat in the regular first-class section of the plane for this transatlantic flight, the four boys were treated a bit better than ordinary first-class passengers. They were able to see a film they had chosen themselves, a film that had been specially flown to London the day before their departure.

In New York there was some uneasiness among the men involved in the tour. Were the Beatles still as popular as ever? Disturbing rumors had been drifting in from the European continent since the spring. In spite of the boys' fantastic success—at that time, August of 1965, more than 100 million single recordings and more than 25 million long-playing disks of the Beatles had been sold throughout the world—in spite of all this, at their arrival in Rome for a concert that spring there had been 150 police on call at the airport and only four docile Beatle fans, and these hadn't even screamed. Concerts in Vienna, during that same tour, were canceled for lack of advance sale.

While reasonably certain that the foreign decline in

Beatle popularity had been caused by an upsurge of groups such as the Rolling Stones, the Dave dark Five, Herman's Hermits, and The Animals instead of a loss of interest in the Beatles themselves, the promoters of the American tour were somewhat uneasy.

Nevertheless all the necessary preparations for minor riots at the airport, in the city, and at Shea Stadium were taken by city police, private police, and hotel police.

These groups began to plan strategic tactics days in advance.

At the Warwick Hotel, where the Beatles would stay at I $302 a day, there was only one elevator to the Governor's Suite on the thirty-third floor, the pad set aside for the four boys. The thirty-second floor of the hotel, more accessible, was reserved for the Beatle entourage, a considerable one.

At Kennedy International Airport, the men responsible for security finally managed to outwit the hordes of fans. When the Beatle plane touched down at 2:35 P.M., only four teenagers were anywhere near the right place, and they had cheated, reaching the area in a Port Authority ; car with Port Authority employee friends.

The officials had managed to have the overseas jet land in a secluded southwest corner of the field, nearly two miles west of the International Arrivals Building.

Although the teenagers at the airport were outfoxed by this maneuver and Were not there to scream and shout as the Beatles set foot on American soil, there were dozens of policemen and about seventy-five photographers and reporters. After the landing, the other ninety passengers on the plane were kept waiting while customs and health officials cleared the Beatles and their party of sixteen. I When the boys finally emerged from the plane, all waving at the newsmen and chewing gum in unison, three Cadillac limousines whisked them off the field and into the city.

Police at the hotel again outwitted the crowds of waiting fans by concentrating all their forces on one side of the hotel. The crowd surged toward that area while the Beatles were smuggled in on the other side, escaping everyone but a few canny fans long familiar with such diversionary tactics.

At the hotel a press conference set up in the Warwick Empire Suite was swiftly packed with over two hundred people. How many were news people and how many were ringers is hard to say, though a suspicious number carried little box cameras and seemed desperately young.

The Beatles, tired from their trip, answered most of the questions with a grunted "yes" or "no." The longer answers were given by John.

"What do you like least about America?" a reporter asked.

"You," John answered curtly.

A woman reporter asked, "How has money changed you?" and Paul snapped back, "It's made me richer."

"Where is your private life easiest, here or at home?"

John answered that moodily. "We don't have any private life here."

"What do you think of Sid Bernstein?"

126

John: "Loved his West Side Story"

"Do you plan to make a dramatic movie?"

John: "No. The only thing we have lined up is Othello."

"Why aren't Paul and George married?"

Ringo fielded this one. "Because John and I wouldn't have them."

Later up in their tower suite, the boys relaxed m a layout containing a living-bedroom unit, two more double bedrooms, one single bedroom, a bar, a small dining room, twin baths, and a rash of closets. The Warwick Hotel telephone operators grew hot and tired as they answered as many as 200 calls a minute, while out m the Streets around the hotel a crowd of 10,000 girls strained against police barricades.

Sunday, at CBS Studio 50, the Beatles taped and recorded six songs for a television tape that was to be shown September 12th on the Ed Sullivan show. During the rehearsal, the studios were assailed again and again by armies of fans, but withstood the onslaught until the Beatles had finished rehearsing and were ready for the performance. This went on before a studio audience of 700, and Sullivan, who M.C.'d it in a stunned fashion, later described it as "sheer murder."

The vigil outside the Warwick Hotel had started Friday night and it proceeded through Saturday and Sunday, the girls waiting futilely, and with ragged impatience.

Some brought their lunches and pelted the police with the remnants when things grew dreary. One long-haired girl in jeans and with a knapsack on her back, broke down in uncontrollable sobs, screaming "Paul, Paul—where are you? I've come all the way from Albany."

But the long day dragged on and it soon became obvious that there was no chance of any of them getting to see the Beatles. Still they waited, crying, shouting, or silently weeping, hoping for some sort of miracle.

Saturday night the boys threw a swinging party in their sky-high suite and at 3.30 A.M. tumbled into bed, ready for the next day at Shea Stadium.

One of the rumors "leaked" to the papers by Tony Barrow, a press agent of the Beatles, was that Paul would definitely marry Jane Asher, although no date was set. Ten waiting teenagers grew hysterical at the thought of losing the "beautiful Beatle" to Jane.

That Sunday night, at an estimated take of one hundred dollars a second, the Beatles performed in a packed Shea Stadium. About 2,000 fans were turned away, but with the fury of rejection they stormed the police barricades, pulled down the wooden barriers, and with a touch of ingenuity turned them into scaling ladders to breach the stadium ramparts. About 50 of them were successful at getting inside.

There was little to hear at the concert, except the noise made by the fans. The performing platform was set up at second base while the audience was restricted to the stands. From time to time the Beatles faced in different directions, and a sudden frenzy gripped whatever part of the audience they were facing. The only silence of the evening occurred when the "Star Spangled Banner" was played before the concert. Afterwards an announcer stepped to the microphone and said "Don't worry, the Beatles are here!" and from then on there were only tears and agonized moaning and screaming.

The sound system was a joke, a droning, muffled beat in the muggy August night. Before the Beatles came on, the audience had to sit through a pastiche of discotheque dancers, loud, hoked up disk jockeys, and pop combos.

When the Beatles finally appeared they were almost lost in the vastness of the stadium. Spots picked them out, but they were hardly recognizable as anything bigger than flies. The screaming grew more shrill and sustained, a massive sonic burst accompanied by weeping, stamping, leaping, and fainting.

Thirteen television cameras, one in a helicopter, recorded the concert for Ed Sullivan as the madness continued. Dozens of hysterical girls were carried from the stands to a first-aid dressing room. After the concert the girls tore down the barricades and sobbed pathetically at the police, "They walked on that grass . . . tear us up some blades, please, please!"

Before the barriers, gave way, a New York Mets station wagon had driven onto the field, up to the temporary stage, rescued the four Beatles and raced away through a left-field gate to a waiting Wells Fargo armored truck, while the crowd screeched in frustration.

The armored truck took them to the nearby heliport at Top of the Fair, where a helicopter bore them aloft and back to the city.

They left an exhausted New York and thousands of girls with laryngitis the next morning. There were seven disk jockeys, one radio news director, two British newsmen, a British radio star, and two reporters on the plane with them. Other hangers-on brought the chartered planeload up to 60 people. Along with the Beatles there were the other groups that shared the concert stage and rounded out the half-hour Beatles' performance to a full-sized concert.

These Included the Sounds, King Kurtis, the Cannibal and the Headhunters, a group of discotheque dancers, and singer Brenda Calloway.

Although the rear of the plane was set aside as a private compartment for the boys and Epstein, at the very beginning of the tour George Harrison, making a strong bid to overcome his reputation for shyness, went through the plane introducing himself to everybody and chatting graciously with reporters and disk jockeys. This became the pattern.

When the boys wanted to talk they'd leave the back section and come forward. Otherwise, they had a regal sort of privacy.

In Toronto, their next stop, they appeared at the Maple Leaf Gardens for two shows, with a press conference in between. The questions asked by the Canadian press had a more serious ring than those the American reporters had asked.

"What do you think of the controversy over your Order of the British Empire?" one newsman inquired.

As usual, John answered. "Lots of people who complained about our receiving the medal received theirs for heroism in the war—for killing other people. We received ours for entertaining other people. I'd say we deserve ours more. Wouldn't you?"

At this conference George, with a straight face, blandly told a reporter, "We don't have an image and we don't believe in images,"

From Canada the plane took them to Atlanta, Georgia, while the four Beatles played blackjack, poker, and roulette with Neil Aspinall and Mal Stevens. Mal was one of their road managers, a close friend who had been with them from the early days. For the roulette game they used a miniature wheel Brian Epstein had carried aboard.

For most of the tour the boys preserved their privacy, keeping a very definite division between themselves and their close intimates on the one hand and the rest of the sixty passengers on the other. They were stars now, no mistaking it, and while they still acted without the arrogance of many stars, they were definitely aware of their own position.

The Atlanta visit was brief, since there was no overnight stay planned. Here, though the fans screamed as loudly as ever, the sound system was better and the boys could actually be heard, probably because John, in great annoyance after the Shea Stadium concert, had argued about acoustics with Epstein and the sound men. "If Americans can send a ship to the moon, then they can surely manage to solve this screaming problem." Solve it they did with some careful engineering, at least in Atlanta.

"How does it feel to sing while thousands scream?" a reporter asked the Atlanta press conference.

Again it was John who answered. "Well, we know all about that from both sides. We played for five years without the screaming, but to tell the truth, we like it better with."

In Atlanta they were also asked, "What do you think of Elvis Presley?" and again John took the ball. "We liked his early stuff, but he's got a bit middle-aged, hasn't he?"

One of the things about the boys that impressed everyone who traveled with them at this time was their seemingly inexhaustible energy. One of the men asked George Harrison, as they left Atlanta, "How do you do it? How do you go on like this with no rest?"

George shrugged. "Well, actually, this is kind of relaxing for us, you know. We enjoy it. In fact, I'm much more relaxed right now than you are."

From Atlanta they flew to Houston, where the same pattern was repeated. Here, however, two hundred teenagers broke through police cordons to storm the plane and climb all over it. The Beatles had to be taken off at the rear emergency exit by the caterer's lift truck. The boys huddled on the platform, nine feet up, while the truck carried them off the field ahead of the howling fans.

In spite of incidents like this, each stop was essentially the same. There were shrieking girls, concerts with barely audible music, press conferences with the same tired questions: What were Paul's plans for marriage? Now that Ringo's wife is expecting, did he want a boy or a girl (answer: "I don't mind as long as it's one or the other"). What did they eat? What did they wear? What would they do when it was all over? The questions dragged on through the long, hot summer,

From Houston they flew to Chicago, where at a press conference

Paul made a peculiarly prophetic suggestion. "People will like us a lot more when we're older, especially older people."

In Chicago they stayed at O'Hare's Sahara Hotel. That night the hotel was filled with teenagers who, suspecting where the boys would stay, had booked rooms in advance They wandered about the halls all night, brazenly knocking on doors and seductively asking each and any member of the Beatle party if they could come in and talk about the Beatles. One of the men named the hotel "Lolita Lodge."

Gradually and inevitably the days became repetitious and boring for all members of the tour. The only break in the predictability of events would come when one or another of the four Beatles did something "naughty" usually at a press conference. In Chicago, Paul shocked the press by sounding off bitterly about segregation in the States.

"I believe Negroes will be in control one of these days," he said. "Then they'll make the white people suffer as they've suffered. It may sound cruel, but it's only natural isn't it?"

Ringo put in his opinion that segregation was a lot of rubbish. "As far as we're concerned," he said, "people are people, no different from each other. We'll never play in South Africa if it means a segregated audience."

At this same session, Paul took off on how shocked he was at the dishonesty and immorality he often ran into in America at high levels. As an example he cited a high police official in Chicago who, that same day, had come backstage and told the General Artists Corporation representative to write out a check to him as a payoff, and make it seem like a tip.

Asked if they intended to pay, Paul shrugged. "Sure we will," he said cynically. "After all, we want to come back to Chicago some time, don't we?"

From Chicago they flew to Minneapolis, to Portland, to San Diego, to Los Angeles, and finally to San Francisco.

In Los Angeles they had about six free days, and they rented a house at Benedict Canyon, a horseshoe-shaped, ranch-style house, complete with swimming pool and patio overlooking the valley below. It was while they were staying here that they met Elvis Presley for the first time.

The meeting was arranged with as much secrecy and maneuvering as a summit conference. Colonel Parker, Presley's manager, went into careful session with Brian Epstein to arrange all matters of protocol, including where, when, and how.

The Beatles, departing from their pose of tolerant boredom, became very excited at the idea of this meeting. They had deep feelings about Presley in spite of their putting him down at the Atlanta press conference. They knew that he was the performer they had first copied in attempting to develop a style, and they felt an empathy and closeness to his original sound. In the beginning they had even gyrated and twisted in a mutation of Presley.

Their road manager, Malcolm Evans, a huge but gentle guy who acted as bodyguard, bouncer, and assistant Man Friday to Aspinall's Man Friday, had been the president of the Elvis Presley fan club back in Liverpool, and now he was allowed to attend the meeting with the boys. Epstein and the press agent, Tony Barrow, also came along, though it was agreed that no news stories or photographs would be leaked to the press.

After a great deal of discussion it was decided to meet at Presley's place. For one thing, the security there was superior to anything the Beatles could get up on short notice.

The meeting, looked forward to so eagerly, was something of a letdown for the Beatles. Presley, handsome and clean-cut to a painful degree, didn't smoke or drink or curse. He was the image of Hollywood health. In addition he was unbelievably quiet, and had nothing to say to the four Beatles.

In turn, they had little to say themselves. Finally they all sat down to a rousing game of Monopoly, played tor real money. Presley gave the boys a box of all his records as a gift.

To Malcolm he gave a jacket he had worn in one of his old movies and to Ringo an old holster. He told the boys how much he liked their music, and in typical Beatle fashion they told him they didn't like his music anymore.

"You should go back to your original sound," John advised. "It was the greatest sound you ever had." After this exchange they all took up their guitars, and jammed while Epstein and Parker discussed the economic angles of managing phenomena, the boys played a series of numbers with Presley. After they left they all decided that he had been a lot more sophisticated than they had expected. "We thought he'd be right out of Nashville country," Ringo mused, shaking his head. "Instead, well, he's just smooth. Those bodyguards all over the house, and he was so immaculate I and quiet ..." A few evenings after their visit with Presley, the Beatles threw a large party at their Benedict Canyon hideaway, a party for all the members of their tour, newsmen, I photographers, and disk jockeys. The house had a path which overlooked a steep cliff with a magnificent view of the canyon below. The cliff below the house was almost vertical, but teenage girls were constantly trying to climb it for a glimpse of the boys. During the party, and indeed during most of the boys' stay at the house, a helicopter crammed with teenage girls hovered overhead, Hollywood's affluent way of Beatle watching. After the party, while the boys were waiting for dinner with the few guests they had invited to stay on, one of the teenage girls finally managed to climb the slops and cling desperately to the corner of the house below the studio. I with its wide picture window. The four Beatles were being taught American billiards by Larry Kane. Maneuvering g for a difficult shot, he noticed the startled and frightened face of the teenager outside the window. She was clinging desperately above the cliff edge, her camera around her (neck, her face filthy with clay, and her clothes torn by the shrubs. He pointed her out to the boys and all of them, terrified that she'd lose her grip and tumble down the cliff, rushed out to her to help her up. "Can you imagine the bad publicity if she fell and was killed," Ringo asked, white-faced.

Inside the house her terror vanished quickly. They gave her a Coke, and plied her with autographs and souvenirs, and then sent her home in a taxi as a reward for fan valor over and above the call of duty.

It was during this stay in Hollywood that Epstein too decided to give a party for the same group of fellow-travelers who had accompanied them on the tour.

Evidently Epstein had taken a long time to accept the fact that newsmen were not out to exploit the boys. He had had some unhappy experiences with disk jockeys in New York, especially one Murray Kaufman, known as Murray the K. Murray the K had tried to coast along on the Beatles' popularity by labeling himself the Fifth Beatle, and it had taken the threat of a lawsuit to stop him, according to Epstein.

By now, however, Epstein had finally relaxed to the point where he could entertain the press and the "good" disk jockeys at his private cottage at the Beverly Hilton Hotel. Somehow, by all reports from the men and women who attended it, it was a stiff, uncomfortable party. Epstein, as one of the newsmen put it, "played a number of records of the Rolling Stones and the Beatles and tried to jive with it, only it wasn't his bit. He had to work at enjoying rock 'n' roll and pop music, and it was never convincing."

At the party he was friendly, but shy, afraid to open up, afraid to talk, as if this just wasn't his world. He was at ease in the business of it, but not mingling with the performers.

A few days later the Beatles made their final U.S. appearance at the Cow Palace in San Francisco. Because of its construction, the Cow Palace was not the greatest place for security, and this performance ended in a riot.

No one knew why or how the riot started, but people broke through the barrier and stormed the stage, swinging Coke bottles and any weapons they could find. It was a strange reaction, not at all the same as the eager fans' desire to touch the boys or grab souvenirs. This was a hoodlum sort of attack with definite intent to hurt.

One man pulled Lennon's hat off, another went for his midsection and missed. Paul was slammed in the eye and the others were roughed up. Malcolm leaped to the stage along with Neil Aspinall, and a flying wedge of newsmen and photographers. In the melee one policeman was knocked unconscious.

The boys, frightened but game, kept trying to play and finally some semblance of order was restored; and as soon as possible the four were rushed from the platform.

It was a bad way to end a tour, and it left a sour taste in everyone's mouth. It also helped strengthen a steadily growing conviction on the part of the Beatles that touring was one hell of a way to make a living, and the sooner they got out of it the better.

JOHN AND JESUS AND AN END TO TOURING

Hope dies slowly and often reluctantly. Although after their 1965 American tour, the Beatles had decided not to do Richard Condon's Western novel *A Talent for Loving* as a film, producer Walter Shenson was still telling the press that the project was "in the discussion stage."

The Beatles, however, were in transition. Back in England they picked up whatever normal threads there were to their lives. Ringo's wife Maureen had been in her last stages of pregnancy during the summer tour. They had bought a London apartment shortly after their marriage, but now they looked around for a home outside of the city.

The baby was born in September, 1965, a healthy boy who was promptly named Zak, to the consternation of their fans and the delight of the other Beatles. It was a properly "Bearish" name.

The house Ringo finally decided to buy was in Wey-bridge, a wooded, hilly, and exclusive suburb about an hour from London by car. It was just down the hill from the house where John Lennon, his wife Cynthia, and his two-and-one-half-year-old boy Julian lived.

Ringo had planned to move in in November, but he hadn't taken the vagaries of builders and decorators into account. It was almost Christmas before Ringo took occupancy of the huge stucco and shingle Tudor-style house, along with wife, baby, a Nanny, four dogs, and two air guns for target practice.

Paul, still a bachelor, had been bitten by the house bug too, and started searching for one at about the same time that Ringo and Maureen moved into theirs.

After the summer tour, George Harrison and Patti Boyd were married, George having the signal honor of being the first groom in recorded history to wear a coat of Mongolian lamb at his wedding. After the wedding they came home and burned incense. It was two and a half weeks before they were free to take off for their honeymoon in the Barbados.

"The great thing about a wife," George announced proudly after the honeymoon, "is that she's your best friend."

George and his best friend promptly bought a large white sunny bungalow with a conservatory and a music room in the same Weybridge area as John and Ringo. He filled the music room with tapes, records, and a jukebox, and he covered the walls with guitars. He "hired a housekeeper, bought a Ferrari and two Minis, forty-eight leather-bound volumes on natural history, and then settled down to married life.

With marriage George began to expand and drift away from the Beatle "good boy" image, he even sampled caviar and oysters—and liked them.

"The natural thing when you get money is that you acquire taste," he said. "I've acquired a lot of my taste off Patti. You get a taste in food as well. Instead of eggs and beans and steak, you branch out into the avocado scene.

"I never dreamed I would like avocados. I thought it would be like eating bits of wax or fake pears out of a bowl when I saw other people doing it. Now I shove them down with the best of them."

John Lennon was a bit less able to accept the new and good life. He viewed change with some alarm and saw it in terms of his own son Julian. He faced the fact that Julian would not be a Liverpudlian, but he wasn't sure he liked it.

"I don't mind him talking in a posh voice," he said, "or even talking like us, but I couldn't bear him to have a London accent. I'm thinking of sending him to the French Lycee."

John added, "I don't think he owes me anything. He certainly doesn't owe me his life, and there's no point in treating him like a little me, because he's not a little me."

None of the Beatle children could possibly become copies of their parents. For one thing, they are growing up in such different circumstances. The three Beatle houses in Weybridge have large gardens, elaborate bathrooms, and, of course, swimming pools. Hardly like the Liverpool in which the Beatles came of age.

Each Beatle has filled his home with his own peculiar possessions. With John Lennon, a gorilla suit and crutches are typical souvenirs. Ringo has a miniature cannon and a stuffed puppy given to him by John.

Maureen Cleaves, writing for the London Daily Standard, called their lives in Weybridge "peculiarly tuneless." Paul is probably the only one who could tell you the date. The others would be hard-pressed to even tell the year, and indeed whether it was day or night. They have little idea of what they did yesterday. They infuriate their wives by telling stories about what happened that end up 'were you there?'

"The wives," Miss Cleaves found, "were rather quiet girls who fit in completely with their husbands' plans."

Calling their marriages ordinary, secure and contented, Miss Cleaves notes that the wives must be prepared at all times to plunge into the looking-glass world of Beatlemania, to dine in London at as late an hour as 2 A.M. and then go to a night club, to always look elegant and lovely as they field reporters' and fans' questions and to entertain any number of people at a moment's notice. A rough job, even for a veteran professional hostess, and yet readily performed by these three girls.

Paul, the unmarried one, began the winter of 1965 with a bit of soul searching. He explored classical music and abstract art and, although he found he didn't like either, he still insisted that both were worth investigation.

"The main thing about things like that, abstract art, I mean," Paul explained, "is getting to it. I think the same thing is true about our music. If you've been brought up on classical music, or if you're older, set in your ways, you don't want to get to know our music. But young people can get to know it because it sort of grows on them and they develop with it, you know?

"I don't think kids want what their parents want, and as I long as the parents tell them not to like it or want it, they ; will want it and like it. "I tend to like anything my dad doesn't like because I think, well, you're old and you're sort of square and I'm a bit more modem than you are."

It was Paul's formulation of the revolt of youth, and he knew that he and the other three Beatles had led that revolt with music. The sound that they were turning out was by no means the sound of the last generation. It was something new and something different and it had affected all of pop music. But it was just at this point that Paul and me others began to think that the different sound alone wasn't enough.

In the States, during their first and second visits, the boys had met folk singer Bob Dylan, and later Joan Baez.

They were impressed with Dylan's music and Baez's quiet devotion to liberal causes.

In the record studios that winter, they began to compare the songs they had turned out with Dylan's songs, and they found their own wanting. They thought their sound was now conventional and their verses so basic and simple that they seemed juvenile.

"We didn't like the idea of going onstage and being very unreal and doing phony songs," Paul said. "We felt that people would like it more, and we would like it more if there were some reality."

They began searching for reality, starting with the works of Dylan, folk singing's angry young man. Lennon subtly began to change his lyrics, not with Dylan's anger, but rather with an attempt to copy Dylan's ability to "tell it as it is." The lyrics of their songs began to reflect their own search for meaning.

In "Paperback Writer," done at that time, they told the story of "a dirty man and his clinging wife doesn't understand."

In just a few lines they managed to capture the frustration of our times. In "Day Tripper" they turned it into a social comment, and sang about a prostitute, admitting she had "jolly good reason for taking the easy way out."

It's unusual and a complete reversal of things for a. group or an artist to' first find success and then begin to question the way of things. Usually the angry young playwright, singer, or novelist becomes successful and then argues that his anger was "lacking in maturity." He is bought off by success and joins the Establishment he has been so valiantly fighting.

The Beatles, on the other hand, found success first and then began to question the very roots of the system that had lifted them up. They were so firmly established in that system that their questioning of it caused them no trouble. Instead, the adult world of intellectuals who had shrugged them off as a teenage fad, suddenly sat up and began to notice them.

Perhaps part of the answer as to how they got away with it was that they were so much the prototype of British youth in the sixties. They created an image that became a way of life in Great Britain. London, as a swinging city was largely a reflection of that image.

But once they had created the image, they managed to step nimbly aside and search for some new identity of their own. They were sick and tired of the Beatles by 1966. The monster they had created was devouring them. That winter of 1965-66, John Lennon said longingly, "If I had enough money I'd retire and wear a beard and comb my hair back forever and not worry about flashing my ego about."

Their song lyrics began to search and inquire. "Nowhere Man," written in 1965, cries out mournfully, "doesn't have a point of view, knows not where he's going to," and searching inwardly asked, "Isn't he a bit like you and me?"

In their search for the new reality, the Beatles inevitably turned to LSD, a drug that promised new vistas opening out of the submerged consciousness of their minds. They had all tried pot, and found it a magnificent way of relaxing during the mounting tensions of their tours.

But pot was only a mildly euphoric drug. LSD was a deeper, more probing experience and a bit more frightening. Whether it was the medical reports on the effects of the drug, or the reaction of society is not too clear, but in 1966 Paul said, "I don't recommend LSD. It can open a few doors, but it's not any answer. You get the answer yourself, but first you have to know the question."

The answers were what they wanted and needed. Their instant success had left them with the firm conviction that nothing was very difficult, that there was no real meaning to achievement, that you arrived at the top of the ladder and inevitably asked, what have I done and why? What does it mean? Where do I go now? I'm at the top, so what?

They had to have an answer to that "so what" and they started searching for it. Money and success themselves were obviously not enough.

"We're not rich anyway, not by rich standards," Lennon said. "Sure, I have a Rolls-Royce, but I couldn't afford to run four Rolls-Royces like people do, or live on eight hundred acres of expensive land. There's just so much money to be earned. I want the money just to be rich. The only other way of getting it is to be born rich. If you have the money, it's power without having to be powerful."

The statement was a put-on, but with bitter overtones to it, for now at least the four had all the money they needed. They could do as they pleased, but they weren't yet sure what to do. As Paul put it, "We always had this little bright Bethlehem star ahead of us, guiding us on. Fame is what everyone wants, but in the end it is only getting out of a parking fine because the bobby wants your autograph, or else it's being interrupted while you eat by a fifty-year-old American lady with a pony tail."

In December of 1965 they took their last British tour. They were about ready to give up touring "but not just yet," they said. In June of 1966 they wrote "Paperback Writer," and in the same month they started their Germany-Far East tour with a completely new set of outfits made for them by one of London's new boutiques.

The new outfits, earning Brian Epstein's vague disapproval, were unusual even for the Beatles. They wanted to break with what they considered tradition, to change their image, and this seemed an obvious way to do it. One of the set of suits made for them had a double-breasted jacket with rows of big corded buttons and corded lapels. These suits were green, and another set was made of a light gray material with orange stripes. Their shirts were crepe with stripes of orange, yellow, tan, and maroon.

The June 1966, foreign tour started in Munich where they found that six pieces of baggage had failed to arrive. In the baggage, of course, were the new outfits, and the new images. .

"What the hell can we do?" Paul kept shouting at Neil and Malcolm. "We can't go on without the suits."

John finally said, "Why not? We've gone without them for over five years!"

Eventually, just before the show, the outfits caught up with them and the new-imaged Beatles tried out some new and old sound, to thunderous applause.

On the train from Munich to Essen they listened to their first copy of the album Revolver, flown in from London. They had waited uneasily for this album, and they listened to it with sighs of relief.

It was a tremendous turning point. The music was a radical departure and the lyrics were deeper, more searching and more meaningful. It was the first answer to where they could go and what they could do.

From Essen they went to Hamburg, and renewed some old acquaintances. They left Hamburg airport to fly to Japan. There was a stopover at Anchorage, where they were forced to wait while a powerful typhoon approached Tokyo and blew itself out. Ten hours later they took off for Tokyo and the last lap of their last foreign tour.

Afterwards they had one month to prepare themselves for what was to be the very last tour of their career, the August, 1966, American tour.

There is very little point in detailing it, for it was much like the others, except that the audiences were smaller. And, of course, there was the tremendous religious rhubarb raised by John Lennon's famous Jesus remark.

He had made the remark months before the tour to Maureen Cleaves, the previously mentioned reporter for the London Evening Standard. His statement was, "Christianity will go. It will vanish and shrink. I needn't argue about that. I'm right, and I will be proved right. We're more popular than Jesus Christ now. I don't know which will go first. Rock 'n' roll or Christianity. Jesus was all right, but his disciples were thick and ordinary. It's them twisting it that ruins it for me."

It was all part of the new searching, the desire to know and to understand the meaning of things, combined with a bitterness at the entire Establishment and its perversion of all religious principles. Reading it carefully, there can be little doubt that it is the statement of a man who, if not a believer, is at least searching for a belief.

Great Britain read Lennon's statement on Jesus and religion and, accepting it for what it was, promptly forgot it. But at the end of July the quote was reprinted with excerpts from Cleaves's interview in a United States magazine for teens, Datebook.

Response in the States was swift. Tommy Charles manager of WAQX in Birmingham, Alabama, banned all Beatle records from his radio station. Station KTEE in Idaho Falls did the same, qualifying the ban with "until Lennon retracts." Station KZEE in Weatherford, Texas, didn't care about retractions. They banned the Beatles forever,

Brian Epstein, sick in bed, pulled himself together and caught a jet for New York on August 4th, a week before the boys were due to start their 1966 tour.

At a news conference at the Americana Hotel, he assured the reporters that the Beatles would not cancel their nineteen-day American tour. He was here, he said simply to clarify the statement John had made. Sweating a bit in the August heat, he insisted that Lennon had been represented entirely out of context by Datebook.

According to Epstein, what John said and meant was that he was astonished by a decline in interest during the last fifty years in the Church of England and therefore in Christ. John didn't mean to boast about the Beatles' fame. He simply meant to point out that the Beatles had a more immediate effect upon the younger generation.

"In the circumstances," Epstein explained, "John is deeply concerned and regrets that people with certain religious beliefs should have been offended in any way."

When asked whether Lennon had denied the article and its contents himself, Epstein said he had indeed done so in London.

"Would John change his remarks?" a reporter asked.

Epstein wet his lips and hesitated, then softly said, "It's highly unlikely."

The tour, he said, would go on as planned. "I have spoken to many of the promoters and most are not anxious that the concerts be changed or canceled."

Memphis, the closest concert spot to Birmingham and reasonably the most likely to be affected by the whole fuss, had sold more tickets the day before the press conference than on any other previous day.

Answering the fact that sales this trip were not as high as they had been on previous tours, Epstein said this was only natural. "They are not the novelty they once were. Figures are as good as I could possibly expect, and in many cases the concerts are sellouts."

Meanwhile, Maureen Cleaves, anxious to help out, told another group of newsmen in London that John Lennon had been reading extensively about religion. "He was simply observing that the state of Christianity was so' weak that the Beatles were better known to many people."

Was it an indictment against people, or against Jesus? Radio Requete in Pamplona, Spain, saw it as an attack against Jesus and decided to play no more Beatle music till it was withdrawn.

However, in Hong Kong, where most listeners were Buddhists, the radio station announced that they would play Beatle records as long as listeners liked them.

"Religious beliefs have nothing to do with an artist's performance—and the Beatles are artists," they said, begging the real question.

Johannesburg, South Africa, however, perhaps remembering the Beatles' statement that they would never play for a segregated audience, banned all Beatle records from their state-controlled radio station. Meanwhile, in America, stations in Kentucky, Ohio, Georgia, Mississippi, South Carolina, Massachusetts, and Connecticut joined the boycott.

On the positive side, station WSAC in Fort Knox, Kentucky, began playing Beatle records for the first time to show their "contempt for hypocrisy personified." The Reverend Richard Pritchard of the Westminster Presbyterian Church in Madison, Wisconsin, said that anyone outraged by the statement should blame themselves, not the Beatles. They should, he said, "take a look at their own values and standards. There is much validity in what Lennon said," he added. "To many people the golf course is also more popular than Jesus Christ."

Even in South Africa a local paper criticized the South African Broadcasting Corporation for its threat to ban the Beatles, although they added that no Christian or agnostic would defend or condone the vulgarity and cheapness of Lennon's remark. But they felt banning was no answer "We suggest that the SABC will not do Christianity any good nor the Beatles any harm if it carries out its threat."

Variety, the ultimate spokesman for show business, granted that the Beatles' box office had fallen off, but thought it unlikely that the religious brouhaha was the reason. On August 10th, they reported, Shea Stadium was only 80 percent sold out for the August 23rd concert. The year before it had been completely sold out two weeks before the concert and thousands were turned away.

Analyzing the fact that box-office interest in the Beatles was waning, Variety speculated that the marriage of three of the boys could be the reason, and went on to suggest that their original fans had outgrown them.

"It will be difficult to find promoters who will be willing to pay them $125,000 per night against 65 percent of the take, as Sid Bernstein is guaranteeing them at Shea Stadium," Variety said.

Nevertheless, the tour went on as scheduled. In London, in a driving rain, the four Beatles boarded a Pan Am plane for the United States as a crowd of 500 fans watched them. One young girl bit her knuckles and cried, "Please, John . . . don't go. They'll kill you!"

Lennon wasn't exactly afraid that they would kill him, but he admitted, "We've never left for America with this sort of feeling before. Frankly I'm worried."

While they were in transit, Mayor William Ingram, Jr., of Memphis, announced that the Beatles' fourteen-city tour could forget Memphis and become a thirteen-city tour. "We're going to protect Memphians against the Beatles' use of the public Coliseum to ridicule anyone's religion!"

Despite the anxieties and the hostilities, the tour proceeded in a normal fashion. After their arrival in the States three girls invaded their plane at Chicago's O'Hare International Airport to steal the pillowcases the boys had used on the flight. Later, at the Astor Towers, 200 screaming teenagers tried to storm their private suite and one girl was severely injured.

At a Chicago press conference, arranged to let John apologize for his religious "put-down," Lennon, obviously nervous and pale and not at all his cynical self, said uneasily, "I do believe Christianity is shrinking, but that doesn't mean that I have un-Christian thoughts. I could have said TV, cinema, or big cars were more popular than Jesus. Sometimes we just forget that we are Beatles and we say things we'd say to a friend across the bar."

Unhappily, he added, "I am sorry now I opened my mouth!"

America swiftly accepted his apology and sellout crowds attended the concert while the Chicago Daily News proclaimed, "Lennon Forgiven: Beatles Mosey on, Richer than Ever!"

With that squared away, they played Detroit, Cleveland, Washington, D.C., Philadelphia; then flew up to Canada to perform again at the Maple Leaf Gardens; then to Boston, Cincinnati, and Memphis, where in spite of Mayor Ingram's pronouncement and a picket line, no incident occurred; then on to St. Louis, New York, and out West to play Seattle, Los Angeles, and wind up on August 20th in San Francisco at Candlewick Park.

By then a feeling of sadness had descended on the entire group. There was no question that this was the last tour. They needed neither the money nor the popularity any longer, but it was still like the end of an era.

Perhaps Epstein felt it most. The boys had a dozen different plans, especially now that Revolver was accepted.

Their future looked bright and exciting but to Brian Epstein, there seemed no future at all.

"What will I do now?" he asked plaintively. "My whole life has been devoted to managing these tours—at least the most significant part of my life. I've neglected my other artists and done everything to concentrate on the Beatles. Not that I've regretted it for a moment—till now.

Now it seems as if I've just come to the end of things.

They can go on, but they don't need me. What do I do now? Where do I go?"

His bitterness and despair grew worse when they returned to England in September. He hadn't even the satisfaction of honestly believing that he had made the Beatles. In truth, they had made him. His management of the four has been referred to as brilliant, but when you've got that sort of a tiger by the tail, you don't manage it brilliantly. You just race along after it, and essentially that was what he had done.

He had made some fantastically high financial demands, which had been met because of the Beatles' popularity, and he had worked at shaping their image, with moderate success. He had tried to manage them with decency and responsibility and with a commitment to their fans, and in this he had been successful. But by no stretch of the imagination could he cast himself in the role of Pygmalion. He had not created this group, nor had he directed it musically, and this, to a man who always thirsted after creativity, was the bitterest pill to swallow.

In addition, his own private life was hopelessly muddled and confused. He had never been able to maintain an intimate relationship with a woman, he just didn't care for them, and yet he felt that the life he did lead only served to degrade him.

The confusion and torment turned him to searching for some way out through pills and drugs and finally, in September of 1966, he was driven to try suicide. This too failed and he went on for almost a year in the same pattern.

For the Beatles the winter of 1966-67 was a time of excitement and growth. John expanded his acting career with a part in the film, *How I Won The War,* while Paul tried his hand at composing music for another motion picture, The Family Way. While he wasn't completely satisfied with the results, it at least was another direction.

Ringo and his wife and baby settled into a comfortable domesticity. Ringo had never been tormented with the others' restless creative urges. He was satisfied with his performing and his newly acquired bourgeois standing. He lived his life in an ordinary fashion to the accompaniment of a constantly blaring television set. Meals were eaten in front of it, and the housetop was covered with elaborate aerials to pick up all available stations.

Ringo, however, though his own demands were less, went along with the others happily, trying drugs when they did and performing in the new mode they were developing, contributing to the style when he could.

It was a year of idleness in a way, but it would have been hard to find four people more enthusiastically idle than these. John and Ringo made tape after tape, often working far into the night. John began reading in earnest, discovering history and religion.

"I have decided I am a Celt," he said. "I am on Boadicea's side, you know, all those bloody, blue-eyed blonds chopping people up."

He would ask all his friends, or any stranger he met, if they knew of any good books to read. He began to study all the daily newspapers in Great Britain, to watch all television news coverage, and in an old, faded scrapbook he wrote endless poems and stories.

His mother-in-law bought him a novel by Dickens, autographed by the author, and John commented, "I can't stand Dickens' writing, but it's not bad having his autograph, is it?"

Back in 1963, when the Beatles were just coming into their own, George had told about a secret ambition he had had ever since a trip to the Canary Islands.

"I met a Spanish guitarist there who taught me a Sego-via piece," George said. "It was absolutely marvelous, and it opened my eyes to what music can be. I'd love to be able to play a Spanish guitar unamplified, where it sounds like eight people playing at once."

Intrigued with the nuances and possibilities of serious classical guitar playing, he built up a library of recordings of Segovia. "It's almost impossible to find the time to practice," he had said, "but someday—someday."

Now, three years later, George and Patti could go off to India, where George continued a fascinated exploration of Indian music. The Indian sitar, a fantastically complicated stringed instrument, usually requires a seven-year apprenticeship to learn. Under the tutelage of Ravi Shankar, the expert sitar player, George became extraordinarily adept, and began to introduce the instrument into his music. The record, "Norwegian Wood," has a passage of sitar playing by George.

It's interesting, and typical of George's inquiring mind, that he first encountered the sitar as a prop used in the movie *Help!* He was intrigued by it, just as he had been intrigued earner by the Spanish guitar.

That same winter Paul bought a three-story house in London,

paying £40,000 for the 125-year-old Victorian pile. He continued his "friendship" with Jane Asher, still avoiding marriage, and broadened his exploration of the sophisticated London world of art, theater, and music. "I must know what people are doing," he explained. "I vaguely mind people knowing anything I don't know."

He began to take music lessons and became fascinated by composers like Stockhausen and Beria.

During this period they took a somewhat unrealistic view of their separate destinies. "We cannot go on holding hands forever," John Lennon said. "We have been Beatles as best we ever will be, those four jolly lads. But we're not those people any more. We're old men. We can't go on keeping on top of the pops forever. We still enjoy it, but somehow we feel silly. We can't develop our singing, for none of us can sing in tune. We've got to find something else to do. Paul says it's like leaving school and finding a job. He's right. It is like school, because you have the group to lean on, and then suddenly you find that you're on your own."

As a solution, John said, "What we've got to do is find something we can put the same energy into as we did into being Beatles. That's why I go around taping and writing and painting and all that—the answer may be one of them."

George Harrison summed it up more succinctly. "Being a Beatle isn't the living end!"

But the boys were then, and to an extent still are now, captives of their own mystique. They grew up together, relying on each other during their formative years. Caught in the prison of their fame, their young manhood was spent as four against the world, and they clung together, sought sustenance and comfort, understanding and entertainment from each other.

It was a state closer than friendship and as was noted earlier, perhaps even closer than marriage. They can do without their wives and families, as they did on tour, but they can't really do without each other. They visit back and forth constantly, at any hour of the day or night. They drop in on each other unexpectedly, knowing that they'll be accepted eagerly, not as the world accepts them, not as Beatles, but solely on their own value as human beings.

For this reason they were, in 1966 and early 1967, closer than they had ever been, and all their talk of not being Beatles any longer was simply whistling in the dark.

THE CHANGING PATTERN OF BEATLE SOUND

A RESPITE IN TIME

Very often," John Lennon said, "we all get together at my house in Weybridge, put all our LPs in chronological order on my stereogram, and study the changing pattern of sound."

The Beatles' sound can only be fully understood in terms of this changing pattern. Unlike most performers who hit top popularity at the peak of their performing careers and then either hold that level or decline, the Beatles bit the top at an early stage of their music. As they developed and changed, they swept their fans along with them, and made new converts along the way.

It is worth considering but hard to explain just what these four boys had that was so unusual. Their appeal to teenagers, in the beginning, is not too hard to understand. Music apart, they had images that were similar and yet different. There was something to appeal to every type, John to the intellectual and George to the introvert. Paul was the "beautiful one" and Ringo the "ugly one." They were full of life, witty and often wise—but there were other Liverpool groups just as good, and with the same background.

On a technical level, McCartney and Lennon were, in the beginning, little more than reasonably good amateur composers who were assisted in their rise by the poverty of British pop composing standards.

George Harrison is considered the best instrumentalist in the group, but he is still only a passable guitarist. There are at least a hundred others just as good in Great Britain actually single playings of particular chords.

One unique feature of this special beat was that it was only really effective on an electric guitar with tone controls set for a strong treble, to give a "twang" to the sound. The Beatles also used a four-string electric bass guitar with a tuning set an octave lower than the third, fourth, fifth, and sixth strings of a rhythm guitar.

A typical early Beatle song, "Can't Buy Me Love," written in 1964, has twelve bars of chorus supported by only three simple chords with an odd melodic line of third and seventh notes of the scale flatted. This is very derivative of the American Negro invention, the twelve-bar blues.

In "Can't Buy Me Love," Lennon and McCartney have taken this idiom and translated it into an acceptable English form with sweeter lyrics.

But these were just matters of mechanics and tools. How the tools were used was all-important.

The first phase of Beatle music occurred in the years before they were discovered, the years during which they built their reputation, years of practice and learning, the time just before they hit the Cavern and during their early days at the Cavern. This was their Presley-imitation phase, but their style in this phase was also a function of the material they used. They resembled Presley most when they performed the songs of other composers, composers who worked in the Presley tradition.

The Beatles recording "Roll Over Beethoven" is fear-fully close to Presley. The Beatles recording "I Want to Hold Your Hand," a Lennon-McCartney composition, is distinctly the Beatles, unique and different. The big jump to their second phase is not so much a performing jump as a composing jump. Lennon and McCartney wrote "I Want to Hold Your Hand," and the distinct, melodic echoes are already far from Presley.

This second phase is personified by the music in *A Hard Day's Night* and it lasted until 1964 when they made *Help!*

In this second phase they had taken a musical step forward, but the lyrics were very much the same simplified, almost elemental groups of words that all pop music used at that time.

Actually, they were beginning to find their own musical and emotional way. Some interesting songs came out of this period, interesting in the sense that they hold an anticipation of what is to come. "I Feel Fine," with its prophetic opening chord is one. "She's a Woman" with its unique tempo is another, as is "I'll Follow the Sun" with its folk quality.

John Lennon, discussing this period in their lives, said, "We weren't ashamed of it, and I suppose it was right at the time, but even then something told me it wasn't us. Looking back I can see that we weren't in full control of the music. It was good at the time, but it was something written for a period—a period of our growth."

It was more than the music that they weren't in control of. Their image still held them back. They had been forged into the role of four, rosy-cheeked, jolly lads, and lads like that had no business exploring the ways and byways of reality. They were expected to keep hammering out the "Beatles' beat." They were symbols of the teenagers of the world, and their fans had no intention of allowing them to change, nor did their fans have any sympathy with the new directions they wanted to explore. The tried and true road was good enough. Stick to it.

Not only their fans wanted them to remain as they were, but Epstein also felt that too great an image had been created to "blow it all" on some incomprehensible new format. Anyway, he was just beginning to understand what they were hammering out. He didn't fancy facing up to a change.

However, at the end of the first Beatle tour in 1965 (their second visit to the United States) they had spent half a night at the Riviera Motel near Kennedy International Airport, discussing music with Bob Dylan. They had been tremendously impressed with Dylan and his philosophy, so close to many of their own beliefs, and they had also been impressed with the way Dylan searched for reality in his music, telling things "the way they were." Dylan, who had made it as a rebel, had refused to compromise, and this too impressed the boys. They flew back to England with the seeds of change planted in the fertile soil of their inventiveness.

The film *Help!* was another step forward into a new phase. While it didn't have the New Wave quality of *A Hard Day's Night*, it had an advanced satirical touch all its own. It tried in many ways to shuffle a comic-book style into a sincere comment on reality. It swung out in all directions, attacking organized police forces, scientific research in Great Britain, the state, socialized medicine, and a bewildering number of social wrongs. The music in the film borrowed many elements from classical music. It failed here and there, but the failure may well have been because the film was still tied to the Beatles' fairytale images.

John was still faintly sardonic with a touch of a sneer, while Paul was as charming as ever. George was withdrawn and introverted, and Ringo was the clown.

But there were steps forward in the music and the lyrics. The words to the title song of the film were not quite as probing as the Beatle lyrics were to become, but they did show promise and they even hinted at the Beatles' own dilemma. It began, "When I was young, so much younger than today. ..."

The four were trying to open doors for themselves, musically as well as lyrically. Musically there were some giant steps forward. "Ticket to Ride," in the same film, was more exciting musically than any of their old compositions. It had a completely new combination of divergent rhythms and more than a hint of the delightful melodic variations to come.

It was soon after this that George Harrison, deeply involved with Indian music, used the sitar in "Norwegian Wood" and gave birth to an entirely new genre, "raga rock."

"Yesterday," published in 1965, rapidly became a hit on the adult pop scene, even drawing vocalists such as Frank Sinatra, Perry Como, and Andy Williams to record it. But none of them gave the song the bittersweet lyrical quality of Paul's voice singing to the accompaniment of a string octet, a novel and effective background of violins and cello that started still another genre, "baroque rock."

"Yesterday" was a more sophisticated ballad than any that they had written before, and the melodic line is free of the annoying predictability of most pop songs.

The harmony in "Yesterday" too is more advanced going far beyond the three chords of "Can't Buy Me Love," and it uses a sophisticated technique to provide shifting tone colors around the melody. The second bar of the main strain shifts from the major into the relatively minor key, and suspended chords are used, notes held over from one chord to the next.

The total effect is dreamlike, and it signals the end of another phase. The album Rubber Soul was released on

December 6, 1965, and it shattered the fairytale images of the four Beatles for all time.

In Rubber Soul, a Lennon pun, they turned away from the percussive, electronic background of rhythm and blues to more intricate and subtler forms. Of the lyrics in the album, Paul said, "You can't be singing fifteen-year-old songs at twenty, because you don't think fifteen-year-old thoughts at twenty."

Indeed, the lyrics were far from fifteen-year-old lyrics, and a bit more sophisticated than twenty. No one had done more than smile at their earlier lyrics. "I Want to Hold Your Hand" was sweet enough, and even the words to "I Saw Her Standing There" ("She was just seventeen, you know what I mean"), were hardly enough to cause a raised eyebrow. But in Rubber Soul, John wrote "Girl" after reading a book called Pain and Pleasure, and he based the theme of the song on the "Protestant ethic of work."

In view of what went before, the lyrics of "Girl" are fantastic. For example: "Was she told when she was young that pain would lead to pleasure?"

Suddenly, and with breathtaking clarity, John Lennon emerges as a man. The jolly lad is absolutely gone. The "mirror is cracked from side to side." The image lies in cold shards of glass reflecting the baroque buttresses of a dreamlike Camelot.

On the record, as John sings "Girl, girl, girl..." with a peculiar in sucking of his breath, the electronic manipulation of sound can be heard in the simulation of a percussion instrument, a repeating rhythm that is enormously effective.

The bewildering thing about the album, to the teenager at least, was the sudden subordination of the Beatle beat. Instead, an unreal melodic quality takes over, a romantic mood reminiscent of old English ballads and angel-voiced medieval boy choirs.

There are startling influences from the past in this music, mixed with a host of contemporary trends, most particularly electronic amplification. When the Beatles started out, electronic amplification was far from new. The blues techniques used it a long time ago, but gradually the Beatles went beyond simple amplification, and began to use and study sound itself. George Martin, who produces their albums, is a genius at sonic manipulation, and he manipulates it every which way blending and dubbing to create an entire new type of music.

In Rubber Soul, sound effects are combined with experimental work in classical music as well as contemporary art music, country music, French popular ballads, gospel, and baroque counterpoint.

For example, m "In My Life," a lovely ode to a modern lady of today, they borrow a bridge from the seventeenth century Baroque period of music, and yet the total effect holds no anachronism. The blending is perfect.

Paul, discussing the album when it appeared, said hopefully, "Our best influences now are ourselves. We are so well established that we can bring fans along with us and stretch the limits of pop."

And stretch them they did, even to borrowing a bit from Donovan, the Irish pop folk singer, to get the misty effects of their later albums. They stretched their own limits as well. "We might write specifically for other people or for different instruments. You name it and it's possible we could do it. I wouldn't mind being a white-haired old man writing songs," Paul said, grinning, "but I'd hate to be a white-haired Beatle playing at, the Empire Stadium!"

THEY WANT TO TURN US ON: A MUSICAL MATURATION

ANOTHER RESPITE

The album Rubber Soul brought the Beatle music into the tricky area of double meanings. You cannot write a lyric to a song using equivocal phrases without running the risk of equivocal interpretations. The song "Norwegian Wood" speaks of a girl who takes the singer to her room. They can't get together because she works in the morning and he doesn't. In spite of John and Paul's insistence that this was the sum of the lyric's meaning, a critic insisted that the song told of a man trying to make love to a lesbian.

As the intellectuals of the music world sat up and took notice of the Beatles, there came an inevitable intellectual analysis of their music as well as their lyrics. Parallels were quickly drawn between the Beatles' music and the works of serious musicians as divergent in style as Carl Orff and Charles Gounod.

Beatle music, critics insisted, had a simplification in its chord sequences that was similar to Orff's Carmina Burana. This simplification consists of such devices as the repetition of a single chord instead of an expected chord sequence, and fragmented instead of fully developed melodies. What a listener expects to be an eight-bar tune breaks off after six bars.

The Beatle theme in "I Want to Hold Your Hand," has been likened to the theme of Gounod's St. Cecelia Mass, and with some justification.

Their style was labeled not only seventeenth century Baroque, but indeed a good deal earlier in its derivation. The Locheimer Liederbuch, dating back to fifteenth century.

They don't have to understand the music if they can just feel the emotion.

"This is half the reason the fans buy our records. Often they don't understand, but they experience what we are trying to tell them."

Paul, searching for the derivation of their new social commitment said, "Bob Dylan is a fantastic composer. At first I didn't understand. I used to lose his songs in the middle. But then I realized it didn't matter. You can get hung up on just two words of a Dylan lyric. 'Jealous monk,' or a 'magic sailing ship' are examples of the fantastic word combinations he uses. I could never write like that, and I envy him. He's a poet."

But Paul tried to write just like that. In a later song, written in 1967 and used on their television film Magical Mystery Tour, a song called "I Am the Walrus," he blended words without continuity of meaning to try and get an emotional rather than an intellectual reaction.

"I am he as you are he as you are me and we are all together ..." starts off the song. Later he swings into lines like, "Corporation teashirt, stupid bloody Tuesday man you been a naughty boy."

There is the edge of a certain symbolism, but really he is just fondling words for the sound of them, and fascinating sounds they make.

Revolver, the critics unanimously agreed, couldn't be topped. What could the Beatles possibly do for an encore?

What they could do, and what they did do, was to top everything they had ever done before, to set the whole world of pop music back on its heels by coming up with Sgt. Peppers Lonely Hearts Club Band (the apostrophe was omitted from Peppers for some obscure reason, perhaps to deny possession).

Pepper was released in the spring of 1967. Their last American tour had taken place almost a year before. They spent a fruitful winter recording and finding themselves, and in the spring they presented America, if not with themselves, at least with a startlingly new collection of sounds. It is altogether fitting and proper, once you hear the Pepper album, that they stopped their touring. The music they produced on this disk was not capable of being produced in a concert setting. It counted too heavily on electronics for its effects, and also on a host of other instruments besides their own.

The theme, or rather surface theme (there are a multitude of themes below the surface), of the album is of an old-time concert given by an old-time music hall band. The songs are a review of contemporary English life, tied back and front by the Sergeant Pepper theme song. It is one of the first attempts to achieve some sort of unity in an album, to wrap it all up in one theme. After the end there's another end, a horrifyingly effective comment on loneliness called "A Day in the Life." It finishes with the words, "I'd like to turn you on," but the listener has been urned on long before the end.

Using the same relentless guitar beat that Dylan used antiphonally to his own voice, they fit the music in Pepper to lyrics that are sometimes satiric, sometimes buoyant, sometimes sad, but always alive and startling.

They admit they were inspired by Dylan, but in Pepper they leave Dylan far behind. They are every bit as good but much stronger, much more compassionate and tender, yet satirical and bitter and unbelievably inventive and experimental.

The songs are far more sophisticated and complex than anything they had done before, and yet none are "hummable." You don't come away from the album singing them.

The song arrangements are incredibly complicated, some dubbed over and over with influences from almost every kind of music. They achieved their effects by literally sparing no expense. A group of George Harrison's Indian friends play the sitar, the tambura, the dilruba, and the less exotic table harp, while some of the singing is backed up by a string octet with harp and harpsichord, some by the forty-one piece Royal Philharmonic Symphony Orchestra.

This orchestra, at the end of "A Day in the Life," produces some gigantic tonal massings that are unique sonic additions to pop music. They build up an ominous, dark background to the concluding lines of the lyrics: "Four thousand holes in Blackburn Lancastershire . . ."

The holes referred to were those made on the moor with poles by the police of Scotland Yard hunting for buried corpses. They would sniff at each hole for the odor of decomposing flesh.

Just about everyone in the music world was turned on by the album except Richard Goldstein of the New York Times, who said, "The overall effect is busy, hip, and cluttered. Like an overattended child, Sgt. Pepper is spoiled. It reeks of horns and harps and assorted animal noises.

"In addition," he concluded, "surprising shoddiness in composition permeates the entire volume. There is nothing beautiful in Sgt. Pepper, nothing real, an undistinguished collection."

Goldstein's was one of the very few dissenting voices. From the classicists to the pop people, almost all were enchanted. Peter Schrag, writing in the Saturday Review, noted that their inventiveness, free play of ideas, and ability to adapt material "not only reproached the conventions, it virtually destroyed them."

Schrag said, "Among all the works of commentary and protest produced by and for the so-called new generation in the English-speaking west, none have turned out to be wittier or more revealing."

The album, according to Schrag, has a thematic unity that ranges from nose-thumbing satire through heavy irony to a depressing end-of-the-world gloom.

"If it says anything at all," Schrag guesses, "it declares that the conventional world of jobs, money, and status is blind, brutal, and destructive, that it is full of people who hide behind a wall of illusion." The album, he concludes, is music, but "surely it is also literature and criticism, a kind of selective filtering back from one generation to another."

Strong words from the intellectual front, and even stronger were to come. Schrag wrote in the summer, and in the autumn of 1967, the Partisan Review set the official intellectual seal of approval on the four boys when editor Richard Poirier labeled Pepper an "astounding accomplishment for which no one could have been wholly prepared." He said, "It therefore substantially enlarges and modifies all the work that preceded it."

Poirier notes with satisfaction that now the Beatles are beyond patronization. "They have placed themselves within a musical, social, and historical environment more monumental in its surroundings and more significantly populated than was the environment of any of their earlier songs. Listening to the Sgt. Pepper album one thinks not simply of the history of popular music, but of the history of this century."

England's intellectuals too discovered the maturity of the Beatles through Pepper. London's Times Educational Supplement wrote that the lyrics "represent an important barometer to our society." It went on to say, "If the record's understanding were reflected in Britain's teachers, our schools might be more sympathetic institutions than some are now."

The intellectuals had discovered the Beatles, but the hard core of pop music critics hadn't forgotten them. Henrietta Yurchenco, in the American Record Guide, said, when the Pepper album came out, "Without question they have extended the popular music language of our time. No longer are they bound by the strict thump, thump, thump of the rock 'n' roll school with which they began. Though a number of folk rock groups have been musically experimental in the past few years, no other has shown the wild inventiveness of the Beatles."

It was a pretty big bandwagon, with everyone jumping on, but the almost unanimous praise was well-deserved. The album was magnificent on a number of levels, and its impression on the pop music scene will be felt for a long, long time, for good or ill. Already singers like Simon and Garfunkel are being accused of deriving too much from Pepper.

The question of drugs has been raised time and again in connection with the Pepper album. Just why, it's hard to know. The Beatles have made no secret of the fact that they have taken LSD and pot. The Pepper album is drenched in drugs. The very first song, after the Sgt. Pepper introduction, is a straight out-and-out drug song, probably referring to pot.

"I get high with a little help from my friends." The "help" of course is not only affectionate support, but marijuana, offered by the friend.

"Lucy in the Sky with Diamonds" has been knowingly assessed as LSD inspired, though Lennon denies this and insists the title was suggested by a drawing his son Julian brought home from school.

This may be so. Certainly they used the line, "Lucy in the sky," in "I Am the Walrus," but even if Lucy was a creation of Julian Lennon, it's ridiculous to think John and Paul were not aware of the LSD initials in the tide. Certainly they were talking about an LSD trip, instead of a trip down the river in a boat when they wrote, "Picture yourself in a boat on the river, with tangerine trees and marmalade skies." The use of the foods to give descriptive richness is an LSD image, as is the "girl with kaleidoscope eyes." For pure sound this is, incidentally, an exquisite line, and it's no coincidence that she's last seen "there at the turnstile." The motifs of a physical trip, "a boat on a river," a "train in a station" are heard everywhere.

But it is all lovely. Even the porters are a joy to hear, "plasticine porters with looking glass ties ..."

Drugs are also obvious in the song, "Fixing a Hole." "I'm painting my room in the colorful way and when my mind is wandering, there I will go ..."

For that matter, the album closes with, "I'd love to turn you on."

There is really no need to go on in this vein. If they used drugs to "expand the mind," to gain more "insight," or for whatever reason, it is no concern of the listener. The results are what count.

Van Gogh was considered a madman, and knowing psychiatrists point to the psychedelic qualities of his color and design to show he was entering a schizoid stage when he painted his most effective and important words. However, the thing to remember is that they were important works. Who cares if Van Gogh was mad, except as an historical curiosity? Who cares if the Beatles take drugs as long as they produce moving music?

In a talk about physical disabilities, drugs, and art, John Lennon said, "All the great artists had physical disabilities. Byron had gout, Beethoven was deaf, Coleridge took drugs and so did Poe, and Shelley drowned."

"Was that a disability?" Paul asked him innocently.

"It was—after he drowned," John snapped back.

Paul, grinning, went after his point. "What about Coleridge? You said he took drugs. I know he wrote under the influence of opium."

"That was an incentive, not a disability," John corrected himself.

"Drugs can be an incentive," Paul agreed, "but they can also clarify symbolism. They said 'Mr. Tambourine Man' was about a junky. Personally, I think you can put any interpretation you want on anything, but when someone suggests that our 'Can't Buy Me Love' is about a prostitute, I draw the line. That's going too far."

"Sure, and when they say 'A Yellow Submarine' is about pills it's just as silly as saying 'Puff the Magic Dragon' is about a junky."

"Let's examine Jack and Jill more closely," Paul said thoughtfully. "We might find some very suspicious holism there."

The fact that drugs are important to their music is probably behind the fact that the Beatles are now very active in an attempt to legalize marijuana in England. Perhaps, if drugs arouse such a disturbing reaction in most of us, we should consider the Beatles' songs as ways of taking "trips" without drugs. Listening to the songs, the Beatles tell us, is just as effective as taking the actual trip.

But apart from the "yes or no" of drugs—and it is ridiculous to suppose the boys would come out and say, "Yes, we meant drugs by such and such a song"—apart from this, the lyrics to Pepper go far beyond those in Rubber Soul and Revolver.

"When I'm Sixty-Four" is their geriatric salute. They keep the lyrics deliberately trite throughout: ". . . Will you still be sending me a valentine ..."

It's all deliberately cliché until the rather chilling end where the sentimentality of the faded valentine is converted to the pathos of the lonely hearts newspaper advertisement. "Drop me a line stating point of view . . . give me your answer, fill in a form."

Perhaps the most bitter and critical song in the album is "She's Leaving Home," a song which has, incidentally, been attacked by adults for encouraging teenagers to run away. It's hard to see what encouragement there is in a line like, "She's leaving home after living alone for so' many years."

It's the world of adults, the parents, who could best learn from this. The song gives a heartrending cry for all the over-affluent children. "Fun is the one thing that money can't buy."

Is it any wonder youth has looked on the Beatles as its spokesmen?

One last word about Pepper concerns the cover to the album, a photo montage in true Beatle style. The four Beatles, in gaudy satin military band uniforms and vigorous mustaches, are standing above a cemetery-like flower arrangement that spells out BEATLES under a border of what looks suspiciously like Cannabis sativa or marijuana plants.

Sixty-two figures are grouped around the four Beatles and represent the derivative qualities of the Beatle music. For the most part, the sixty-two are men and women who' have urged escape of one sort or another. They range from Bob Dylan through Edgar Allan Poe, Oscar Wilde, Mae West, Marilyn Monroe, Marx, Jung, Lawrence of Arabia, Lenny Bruce, Stockhausen, Aubrey Beardsley, William Burroughs, right down to Johnny Weismuller and Shirley Temple.

It has all the quality of a funeral group watching four bodies being lowered into a common grave. Is it how they see themselves? But standing next to them are the old Beatles, four figures from Madame Tussaud's Wax Museum.

The past is at one with the present, the cover says, and the Beatles have developed out of a multitude of other people's works and creations.

TRANSCENDENTAL MEDITATION AND THE MAGICAL MYSTERY TOUR

SPRING TO WINTER:

1967 Early in the spring of 1967, while the Beatles were finishing up their recording of the Sgt. Pepper album, Paul McCartney, who had been fretting about what they would do next, came up with what he considered an inspiration. They would make a television film. This would kill three commitments with one show. It could be filmed as a movie, released as a television show, and eventually made into a record album.

"The whole thing will be a mystery to everyone," Paul told the other three Beatles as he outlined the project. "Maybe it'll even be a mystery for us too. That way it's sure to be more exciting."

What they would do, Paul explained, was get on a bus with a gang of people, friends and characters, and just drive somewhere, anywhere, taking a sound and camera crew along. They would play the whole thing by ear, doing whatever came naturally. Neither the Beatles, the driver, nor the passengers would know what they were doing or where they were going. In that way it would be mysterious.

"Best of all," Paul said, "we won't need a script. After all, it's just an hour TV show. We'll film like crazy, cut it to an hour, and use our songs for background music. How can it go wrong?"

The others agreed that the concept was great. It would answer the clamor all their fans were making to "show yourselves." They didn't want the boys just to produce recorded songs. The fans wanted the Beatles as well as the Beatle music.

The project would also give them a chance to get their fingers into moviemaking. One of the reasons they had become disenchanted with moviemaking was their own lack of control. At first it had all been new, unusual, and exciting. They had done as the director wanted, posed and acted when they were told, but the total effect was confusing. They hadn't understood what the director was after until they saw the finished film.

How much more fascinating it would be to direct their own movie, plan it and know where it was going and what they hoped to accomplish. With the filmed television show, the mystery tour, all this was possible.

In the excitement over the idea they stopped working on the Sgt. Pepper album for one evening in April and recorded a "signature tune" for the new project. Paul and John worked up a first line, "Roll up, Roll up, for the Magical Mystery Tour." It was a little less than inspired, but then the tune, too, was pretty ordinary.

They spent about six hours recording the first track of the theme and first line of the song. As Ringo tells it, the only exciting thing about that session aside from Paul's enthusiasm, was John's costume. He wore an orange cardigan, purple velvet trousers, and a sporran to keep his cigarettes in.

After that one evening they went back to work on the Sgt. Pepper album. When that was finished they still put off the "Mystery Tour." Perhaps it was lack of excitement over the project or perhaps it was the fact that they discovered transcendental meditation that summer.

The Beatles had been fascinated with India for a long time. George Harrison had introduced them to its music and to the sitar playing of Ravi Shankar.

Shankar's music, while boring and monotonous to most westerners, is unbelievably melodic. Melodies spin out interminably. This melodic quality is one of the most fascinating aspects of Indian music and was adapted by the Beatles to their own style.

Their involvement with the music led them inevitably to an involvement with other aspects of Indian life, the colorful and esoteric aspects—and the philosophy. What attracted them is not hard to understand.

At twenty some odd years, these boys bad everything. They had reached success in the field of music, and then had overreached it by changing their style and still carrying their audience along with them. It seemed all very easy, very smooth—and very meaningless to them.

After you've hit the top, where do you go? Not down, if you're strong enough and talented enough, but there must be some meaning to staying up there. There must be some answer, but if so it was an answer that they hadn't yet received.

They searched for a solution in their creative work, but creative success never answers the need that drives the artist to it. It was foreordained that after trying drugs to expand their consciousness, to expand the limits of reality, they would look for other means of expansion, other answers. The philosophy of the east, though they had ridiculed it a few years before in their movie *Help!* still seemed a possible solution.

The brash and swaggering Beatles of the earlier image could well joke about such mystical answers, but the new-image Beatles had to take it seriously. They had given up the uniforms of their early tours, the Cardin jackets, and even the far-out boutique outfits of their last tour. Now they wore satin, flowered shirts, Beatles and velvet suits, extravagant tunics and pants and affected long, full mustaches.

Along with the new look they began to study Yoga, sparked by Harrison's interest in Indian music. Yoga was interesting, but it wasn't what they were looking for.

That August, in 1967, the Beatles, accompanied by their friend, Mick Jagger, one of the Rolling Stones, attended a public lecture given by an Indian philosopher and mystic, Maharishi Mahesh Yogi. After the lecture the Maharishi invited the four Beatles to accompany him on his coming trip to Bangor in North Wales where he was taking a group of his converts for a bank holiday.

At one stage in their development, they would have been quick to discard the Maharishi's philosophy as arrant nonsense, the fuzziness of a man too far away from the basic necessities of life to do anything but explore its unreal aspects.

However, their own exploration of unreality through I drugs made the Maharishi's lecture seem wise and profound.

The Maharishi, a small frail man with shoulder-length gray-streaked hair and a gray beard, was given to much smiling and unaccountable bursts of laughter in his resonant, but high-pitched voice.

"Life is a homogeneous whole. It consists of spiritual values and material values," the Maharishi told the Beatles. "Consciousness of self has to be found because without inner spiritual values, the ordinary physical and material pleasures which life offers cannot properly be enjoyed."

However, lest he be considered the kind of ascetic who eschews material comforts, the Maharishi made the record clear. "There is no use denying yourself things just for the sake of it. That is not a philosophy of life."

Like many another extravagant personality, the Maharishi had achieved his first fame in Hollywood. In 1959 he left a "life of secluded meditation" after thirteen devoted years. The death of his master, the

Guru Dev, had impelled him to go forth and give himself to the world as an act of self-sacrifice, and Los Angeles seemed a logical place to start the sacrifice.

He stayed there five months and established the Spiritual Regeneration Movement. He had only 20 members to start with, but nine years later he headed an organization with centers in 50 countries and a membership of 150,000.

The Maharishi only charged for his services because "people tend to put no value on what they can get for free." Students therefore paid a minimum of thirty-five dollars to be initiated into transcendental meditation, while adults paid a week's salary. In the case of the Beatles, a week's salary is no mean initiation fee.

In addition to the cash, every neophyte must bring to his initiation six fresh flowers, a new white handkerchief, and two pieces of fruit. He must also be off psychoanalysis and mind-warping drugs such as LSD.

The basic concept behind Transcendental Meditation, the Maharishi's philosophy, is that man is not born to suffer. This is in contrast to Christian theological teaching, The Maharishi says, "Men live and die in the realm of relative multiplicity, binding themselves to illusion, darkness, and pain."

However, he promised that "beyond thought and matter there is an absolute unity which is the basis of all creation. At its ultimate level this constitutes truth, light, and joy."

This level, the Maharishi maintains, exists in every man's consciousness, and if you can reach it for a half hour or so a day, you more or less have it made.

The road to this level, according to the Maharishi, is an old technique lost to the world, but brought back to it now by him. The mind, in meditation, follows a simple word or sound through increasing levels of consciousness to absolute unity, a state of "unknowable bliss."

The Beatles thought they might just like to get to this bliss and perhaps could find it on the weekend with the guru. They accepted his invitation to "come along and meditate" in Bangor, North Wales.

It was to be a secret weekend, but at the very beginning, as usually happens when the Beatles travel, chaos descended and the "quiet" trip was overwhelmed by crowds.

Ringo's wife was expecting their second baby, but he went along anyway at her insistence. Cynthia and John Lennon put off a trip to Libya just to' go along with the rest.

On the train to Bangor, the Maharishi had a compartment to himself. He sat there in the Lotus position, on a white sheet, received supplicants, and dispensed "gems" of eastern lore.

Bangor swarmed with crowds of teenagers who had gotten wind of the Beatles' involvement, but somehow the four got through unharmed to the local university where three hundred followers of the Maharishi greeted them with flowers and bewildered apprehension at the crowds.

During the long weekend, the Beatles listened to the Maharishi, became enchanted, meditated transcendentally, and eventually agreed to follow him to India in September.

After the weekend they decided to get to work on the television film, the Magical Mystery Tour, but they had hardly started when the entire project was made meaningless, at least for the moment, by Brian Epstein's death.

Death or suicide? That was the great question. Epstein was found dead behind locked doors and a dozen different rumors spread immediately, ranging from murder to suicide, including drug addiction, death by an overdose of heroin, death from liquor, and death from pep pills.

The final, official decision, was that his death was due to an accidental overdose of sleeping pills. The coroner at the inquest said, "The post mortem shows the cause of death was carbital poisoning." Carbital is a common sleeping pill. The pathologist failed to find any drugs other than this in his body, despite careful analysis.

No alcohol was found, but there was a trace of a mild tranquilizer. "Heroin, morphine, and amphetamine can be ruled out in this case," the coroner said. "But his blood showed that he had been taking carbital over a considerable period of time. His death was caused by a small, fatal dose of this, and not a massive dose."

The report suggested that he might have become careless or less cautious in taking the carbital, an ingredient of sleeping pills. It also summed up his death by concluding, "Piecing together all the evidence we have a picture of a man who was sensitive, inclined to be anxious, and who had a lot of trouble with sleeping."

It's a restrained view and doesn't take into account the suicide attempt little more than a year before. Brian Epstein was not only sensitive and anxious, but also a deeply unhappy and confused man.

The Beatles were shocked, but not completely surprised by Epstein's death. There had been warnings before and other accidental overdoses of pills. They knew the extent of his depression and half-feared, half-expected this to happen.

They spent the day before the funeral visiting his mother who had been widowed recently, but they did not attend the funeral. They were asked not to, in order to keep it from becoming a "circus to view the Beatles." They agreed to this family request, and Epstein was buried quietly with only the immediate family attending.

In addition to the funeral, Brian's mother arranged for special memorial services in St. John's Woods synagogue. These services were attended by the boys, Ringo, in a conservative black suit with an enormous violet tie, George in a formal, double-breasted suit of black velvet, and Paul with a multicolored scarf knotted over his tie. It was colorful, but their own brand of mourning attire.

The Beatles had planned a two-month break to begin with the trip to India in September to visit the Maharishi and absorb a bit more of his philosophy. Brian's death changed their plans, and they postponed the Indian visit. White Brian's thirty-one-year-old brother Clive began to' pick up the pieces of the NEMS Enterprises, the Beatles looked around for some project to finish up before they left for India.

The Magical Mystery Tour was dredged up again, and the theme song was considered carefully. As far as they could tell, it still held up and needed only some mild reworking.

Paul had dreamed up the thing he called a "scrupt" which was simply a sketch of a circle, representing one hour of television time, divided into eight pie-shaped segments; scribbled notations around the side and in each segment indicated what would happen during the show.

"Hire a coach, yellow!" Paul scribbled on the bottom of the sketch. John gave some thought to the different people who should ride on the coach, and came up with Nat Jackley, an English, rubber-necked comedian; George Claydon, a dwarf; Jessie Robins, a fat lady; and a flock of fan club secretaries taken along as a reward for devoted public relations work.

"Wouldn't it be a great idea to fill the bus with people and get them all drunk, including ourselves and then shoot it."

In the end they decided to hire the bus, which the NEMS organization did for them, and "just go."

The bus that turned up was a good-looking yellow and blue monster with luminous posters glowing from its sides and back. They left from London's Allsop Place, which is the traditional taking-off place for one-night stand pop tours. It was also the place from which they had left on their first British tour.

And last but not least, Allsop Place is near Baker Street, Madame Tussaud's Wax Museum, and the Planetarium, a mess of symbols that appealed to the boys.

There were forty-three people on the bus as it left London and headed toward Devon on a whim of Paul's. "I haven't been to Devon since George and I hitchhiked there a million years ago. Besides, we want this whole thing to be impulsive."

It was more than impulsive. The first two days of the trip were a shambles. The lack of planning told heavily and the impulsive, "let's do whatever comes into our minds" began to wear thin. The three cameramen they had hired were completely bewildered. No one had told them that they'd be shooting on a moving bus with hand-held cameras and no proper lights, and they were horrified at the prospect.

One cameraman turned out to be non-Union, and the Union indignantly threatened to sabotage the whole project. Flustered, Paul offered to pay the man's Union dues, but in the end he had to leave.

Their plan, if it could be dignified by so organized a word, was just to shoot everything and hope for enough funny footage to piece together an hour of television time. "What anyone said, that would be the script," Paul explained. "Whatever anyone decided to be, that was his part."

The fat lady decided to be Ringo's aunt, and sat with him, arguing constantly. It was all very impromptu. In a hotel during a lunch stop they saw some pretty girls sunning at the pool. Jackley, the comedian, started chasing them in Marx Brothers' fashion, and the cameramen quickly filmed it.

The cameramen were beginning to get the hang of what Paul wanted, and under the direction of all four Beatles, they began to film whatever "happenings" happened to happen.

Paul, who was a frustrated director, did most of the directing. When the week of disorganized traveling and shooting was over, he began to search for sight gags to stretch the long, but thin material they had gathered.

He hired a mob of dwarfs, actors dressed as vicars, parents with baby carriages, and football players, put George and Ringo into gangster uniforms and had the entire crowd chase them back and forth across an empty airfield.

As a director, Paul was ahead of avante-garde. He told neither the actors nor the cameramen what he wanted, but tried to create an air of spontaneity by having the actors do whatever came into their heads and the cameramen film it..

Not enough came up, and they viewed the rushes dejectedly and decided that the best stuff had been shot from the window of the bus, involving none of the people they had hired.

In the end they turned up ten hours of filming, and Paul decided he would work with Roy Benson, the film editor, to trim it down to one hour.

Originally they had planned a week for the shooting, a week recording, a week looking at the rushes, and a week editing. Editing alone took eleven weeks, and the total time to prepare the film was fourteen weeks, with a cost of £40,000, double their expected budget.

They had been such babes in the woods about the whole thing that they never realized that more than one take of every scene is a must in moviemaking, or that a variety of angle shots can help to relieve the monotony.

They were raw, but inventive. Mal Stevens, one of their road managers, was a giant of a man with a large stomach. They projected one scene on Mal's stomach and filmed it.

For one of the songs, "The Fool on the Hill," they could find no suitable footage, so Paul decided to go off to France to film background material. He managed it somehow, in spite of the fact that he muddles through his broken verse, and then as the words fail, a wild calliope-like type of electronic jiggery-pokery carries the music away as the singer sighs, "Nothing to get hung about—strawberry fields forever."

THE FUTURE STRETCHES OUT

WINTER TO SPRING: 1968

With the Magical Mystery Tour under their belts, the Beatles settled down to a few months of following their separate interests, though all four turned up with their womenfolk for the opening of How I Won the War with John in a feature role.

John and Cynthia brought Ringo and Maureen to the opening in John's psychedelic Rolls-Royce. Ringo had just returned from Italy, where he had finished with his part of the Spanish gardener, Emmanuel, in the film Candy.

Paul, in a black velvet suit, arrived with Jane Asher, while George, heavily mustached, wore a brocade jacket and silk scarf and escorted his wife Patti, dressed like an "old-time movie queen" in a slit, ankle-length skirt.

Clothes, far-out and colorful, seemed more and more to be the Beatles' particular "bag." They dressed in garish outfits, sometimes with tongue-in-cheek, "look at me" attitudes, sometimes quite seriously. The clothes signified a host of things, not only nonconformity, but a deep symbolism and a means of tampering with their own self-images.

"We are not what we seem," they would say, and prove it by wearing the most unusual, garish outfits they could find. "Are we what our clothes show, or is there a reality within us that no costumes can obliterate?" Hair too has played a part in the identity charade. Sideburns have given way to beards and beards to mustaches. Hair has been worn long or short, in bangs or swept back, while the clothes have teetered between modern and medieval, military and mystical, all part of a kaleidoscope of self-discovery.

Part of the kaleidoscope was Paul's construction of a "deep think" dome in his backyard garden. The dome, resembling a flying saucer from outer space, is soundproof and can be revolved. It has a thirty-foot arch and opens up for stargazing. It was, Paul allows, part of an attempt to get in tune with the infinite.

Drugs hadn't tuned them in completely, but Paul was sure meditation would, either in his new dome or through the help supplied by the Maharishi. "If we had met the Maharishi before we tried LSD," he said enthusiastically, "we wouldn't have needed to take it at all."

While Paul was building his dome, George Harrison and Patti flew to Los Angeles to attend a Ravi Shankar concert and then took a brief visit to Haight-Ashbury to see if the hippies would turn them on.

To some degree they did. He and Patti strolled through Golden Gate Park followed by a crowd of barefoot, flower-decked hippies who showered them with blossoms and peace buttons. George wore a flowered satin jacket and Patti a dress with Indian (American) Beatles.

At one point George was offered a guitar and gave an impromptu concert, then talked at length with the crowd. Afterwards, somewhat wonderingly, he said, "It was all really great. I wonder if it's always like that?"

After he returned to England, he and the other three boys spent the rest of that autumn of 1967 in even closer involvement with the Maharishi. Even nonintellectual Ringo was fascinated by his teachings.

"The four of us have had the most hectic lives," Ringo said. "We have got almost everything money can buy, but when you can do that, the things you can buy mean almost nothing after a time. You look for something else, for a new experience. It's like your Dad going to the boozer, and you want to find out what the taste of drink is like. We have found something new which fills the gap. Since meeting His Holiness I feel great."

George, explaining just what His Holiness preached, said, "The idea is to transcend from the level of everyday thought to the level of higher thought. The value of meditation is to rid your busy brain of all the trash and unnecessary words that constantly inhabit it. Once your mind is clear, you will find yourself capable of thinking on a higher level about things that are truly important, like caring, giving, and loving."

John interpreted it as essentially different from all psychedelic experiences. "The thing is not to drop out, not at all. It's to' drop in, to lose the old, established narrow concept of life and try to make as many changes as possible. Drop in and try to influence as many people as you can to replace hate and fear with love and friendship. You can only do this if your head is clear, your heart is open, and your spirit giving."

Maharishi nodded, giggled at their understanding, and gave his own transcendental view. "Each young person is presented with the beautiful gifts of life by the generations which have preceded him or her. He or she should enjoy these gifts and this life to the maximum, and, in return, he

171

I or she must make his or her contribution toward advancing the glories, goodness, and pleasures of this present life and the life of those who come after him or her."

In the meantime the year rolled to a close, and EMI Records revealed that as of that autumn, the international sales figures for Beatles' disks amounted to 206 million records.

It was enough to pay for quite a few round-trip fares to India, and the four finally took off for their long-delayed visit.

In India, about 125 miles north of Delhi, and across the Ganges from the holy city of Rishiki, lies the religious settlement of Swarag Ashram. Beyond the settlement, in a bit of forest land, is the compound of the Maharishi Mahesh Yogi.

The holy men around Swarag Ashram are as thick as flies, and they live in picturesque poverty, in shacks and caves or out in the open. The Maharishi, however, lives in a degree of comfort most unusual for a simple, holy man. His home, a good-sized brick building, is set round with barbed wire and guards, either to keep the meditators in or the curious out.

The Maharishi decor leans heavily toward silk and antelope skin, bamboo and flowers, though it includes a fair sprinkling of western artifacts.

When the Beatles arrived, the community lost whatever secluded aspects it once had. In addition to any curiosity seekers who could get to this distant outpost, there was a swarm of reporters and photographers.

The four Beatles, their three wives and one girl friend were able to find some privacy within the barbed wire of the compound. When they did join the other disciples of the Maharishi, from whom they ordinarily kept a discreet distance, they came in their own conception of transcendental garb; one in orange- and black-striped pants, one in black velvet, and the two others in white Indian trousers, all with eyelet embroidery shirts and garlands of flowers, Beatles , gold chains, and pendants. Their long-haired wives all wore flowing skirts of sari silk and cotton that reached to the ground.

Actress Mia Farrow, the Irish folk singer Donovan, and a few other celebrities had also come to the Maharishi, their own personal guru, to learn a bit of eastern wisdom to help tide them over the "emptiness of success."

While all four Beatles were sincere enough in their hopes of finding an answer in the teachings of the Maharishi, George with his devotion to Indian music was probably the most deeply interested of the four. It was he who had really persuaded the others to come, and it was he who seemed to get the most out of their sessions with the old man.

Paul and John had an attitude of, "It's really George's bag but we'll try it."

"I get a bit lost when the Maharishi gets into the upper reaches of his metaphysics," Paul confessed.

As the visit wore on, a few others were lost too. Young Mia Farrow took off for a visit to where the "action was," and Jane Asher coaxed Paul to take a little side trip. What a shame, she said, meditation or not, to miss the moonlight on the Taj Mahal.

Ringo, in whom the Maharishi particularly delighted, finally admitted that more than two hours of meditation tended to bore him and Maureen. They were also bothered by the quantities of flies that buzzed over the compound.

He complained to the Maharishi about this and was told that when he became truly concerned with meditation he wouldn't notice the flies. "That's all well and good, but it doesn't zap the flies, does it?" Ringo answered unhappily.

The seeds of discord were planted. "I like the Maharishi," Paul admitted, but reluctantly added, "I just wish he'd talk about the things he understands. He doesn't know much about the draft laws, and I don't think he should defend them."

"He'd do better," John decided, "to concentrate on the simple life. I don't think he should be quite so concerned with material things."

George Harrison had a birthday during the group's visit, and the Maharishi celebrated it in an odd mixture of East and West, seating all the Beatles on a raised platform in front of his other disciples, daubing their foreheads with saffron ochre and ordering the embarrassed George to be deluged with garlands of marigolds while the disciples sang "Happy Birthday to You."

The Maharishi also presented George with a cake, complete with candles topped by a globe of the earth. "This is the world," he told George solemnly. "It needs to be corrected."

During their visit, the Beatles avoided most of the other disciples and as a mark of their distinguished station were allowed as much privacy as they, wanted. They did, however, mix with a few celebrities. George and Donovan hit it off well, and Mia Farrow and John Lennon found that they had youth and success in common, Mia with more of the former and John with more of the latter.

For the most part, although they listened attentively to the Maharishi's "wisdom," the boys found it hard to give up the comforts of their own civilization. They had brought their own food and their own taped music, and they began to practice meditation in their own way.

"We found out that we made a mistake there," Paul said later and John added, "We believe in meditation, but not in the Maharishi and his scene. But that's a personal mistake we made in public. Meditation is good, and it does what they say. It's like exercise or cleaning your teeth. It works, but we're finished with that bit."

To explain why they became involved in the first place, Paul said, "We're as naive as the next person."

John added, "We get carried away with things. We thought he was magic, floating around and all that."

To set the record straight, Paul quickly pointed out, "He's good. There's nothing wrong with him, but his system is more important than the big personality bit. He gets to be treated like a big star, you know."

It wasn't that the Beatles resented the Maharishi's bid for notoriety or his edging into their limelight, but when, early in 1968, he went on tour with another pop group, The Beach Boys, they thought it was a bit too much. Let the shoemaker stick to his last, and the Maharishi's last was philosophy, not show business.

"It's a bit strange, being on the road with The Beach Boys," Paul commented. "Also it folded. You know, that's a silly thing."

Summing up their involvement with the Maharishi, Paul said, "We went to his lecture and we thought, what a nice man. We were looking for that. Everyone is looking for it. We were looking for it that day, and we met him and he was good, you know. He's got a good thing, and we went along with him. Now we're off the train; nice trip, thank you very much."

In the end they departed the Maharishi's scene, showered with his blessings, but uneasily aware that the answer after all, might not lie in Transcendental Meditation.

Where it did lie, they were beginning to suspect, was in work and in their own creativity. This, if handled properly, could well be the key to open an unending number of doors.

Their music had always led them into unique and intriguing pathways. The one thing they were all sure of was that they shouldn't neglect any new paths of this kind that beckoned. But where to go now?

Where they will go can probably be guessed by understanding where they have come from.

Their music, from the beginning, has grown and changed under an influence that has been labeled "contemporary urban." it is urban in the sense that everything was available to them. They have been able to draw from all the urban life with which they have come in contact, as well as from composers like Donovan, Dylan, and Paxton. What all of this has allowed them to turn out is light-years ahead of simple folk music. It is also' light-years ahead of the kind of music everyone joins in singing.

The total effect of the Beatle music, the effect that becomes more and more apparent as they develop, is one of isolation. It is not music designed to be sung by the listener. It is music to listen to, music for an audience, but not for participation. At its present state of development, it is not even concert music. The effects are too elaborate. They can only be produced in a studio.

Earlier music, pre-Beatle music, was designed to reproduce. There was audience participation. Even rock 'n' roll counted heavily on audience participation. The audience danced, moved, responded physically, and above all, sang the songs.

This response was true of the earliest Beatle music, but as they became more involved with sound, more concerned with texture and tone, it became less true. There are still some "singable" songs, but for the most part the trend is toward listening, toward noninvolvement. It is the kind of music people can listen to alone in their rooms with their record players. It appeals especially to the lonely ones, the shy ones.

In a broad sense, this pattern follows the pattern of many young people who are turning away from the world around them, who are turning inward as they are "turning on." It mirrors a concern with drugs as part of a search for some deep self-awareness. It also mirrors a search for meaning in a society that many judge meaningless, or filled with the wrong values.

The hippie movement with its reliance on eastern culture, its reaching toward Zen and its dependence on drugs is all a part of this self-exploration, this trend toward isolation, toward rejection of possessions, success, and society.

Another aspect of the same solitude is today's dancing. Youth no longer needs or wants partners to dance with, no longer achieves satisfaction from physical contact with another human on the dance floor. Watching a couple of youngsters dance today is like watching two individuals taking off in completely different directions.

This isolation, this turning inward exists not only in the field of music and dance, but in literature, in poetry, on the stage, and especially in films. The novelist rums inward and begins to explore his inner self, to lose contact with the world around him in favor of the world within. Saul Bellow's Herzog depicts the ultimate in self-wallowing. On the stage the theater of the absurd rejects all established values and, as in Pinter's plays, sets up minor fantasies in a search for greater inner realities. With Marat/Sade, and later with Hear, the audience is not asked to follow a sequential order of reality and to judge it intellectually, but simply to open their senses to what is happening without logic.

In films, a logical sequence of events is often abandoned in favor of an illogical truth. Kubrick's 2001: A Space Odyssey has its hero travel beyond infinity to turn inward and relive his life in strange, symbolic fashion until he is an enormous fetus in an amniotic sac gazing down at the earth. It's beyond understanding, unless one looks deep within himself, forgets story, forgets obvious logic and reality, and succumbs to the search for greater reality.

This technique has been evolving for a long time in art where painters have gone from representation to abstraction and finally to nonobjectivity, pausing at surrealism along the way, all in an inward search carried to a point where they have become so involved with their own symbols, their own personal portents, that they have lost all sight of the audience. Follow them or be damned, they are off to explore their own souls.

So too, the Beatles turn inward with their music, and happily the inwardness is worth following, for even as they become more depersonalized, more involved with electronics and subtle shades of sound for sound's sake, they express the paradox of turning back in time to a greater personalization. They go to the past to dredge up old Shakespearean strains, seventeenth century music, early English music hall tunes and blend them all together with words that bitterly or sorrowfully or even lovingly expose the dehumanization aspects of our society.

In the midst of this, even while they turn inward and explore their own souls, as most contemporary musicians do, they draw upon the East for the antithesis of our conventional music, the spinning out of melody to incredible lengths, to the utter amazement of our ears.

Where then are they headed? Where now? Well, it's always been change of one sort or another.

"You see," Paul said, "everything changes, so we change as well, and our audience changes as well. We can't put our finger on what age group we appeal to or why. Everything changes, and us too. When we first started, we had leather jackets on, caps, and big cowboy boots. But then we changed to suits. We lost a whole lot of fans, you know. They all said we'd gone posh. They didn't like it because we were all clean, so we lost that crowd. But we gained all the ones who like suits. That sort of thing keeps happening. We lost a lot of people with Sgt. Pepper, but I think we gained more."

"Will we top Sgt. Pepper John mused. "It's the next .move. I can't say yes or no. But I think so, why not? Pepper is only another LP record album. It's not that important."

"We haven't really started yet," George Harrison answered for all of them. "We've only just discovered what we can do as musicians, what thresholds we can cross. The future stretches out beyond our imagination."

INDEX

A Hard Day's Night, 83, 91, 93, 94, 95, 105, 109, 110, 111, 112, 150, 151

Althan, 117

Archer Winsten, 113

Astrid, 43, 44, 46, 53

Beatlemania, 7, 15, 67, 86, 87, 106, 108, 116, 137

Brian Epstein, 4, 8, 9, 11, 13, 49, 50, 55, 66, 74, 82, 85, 86, 95, 129, 132, 140, 141, 144, 166, 167

Can't Buy Me Love, 12, 149, 152, 160

Chicago Daily News, 144

Christian, 143, 144, 165

Cynthia Lennon, 64

Day Tripper, 138

Ed Sullivan, 7, 8, 13, 127, 128

Elvis Presley, 7, 13, 21, 22, 27, 48, 85, 88, 91, 130, 131, 132

Establishment, 20, 76, 92, 110, 124, 138, 141

Forest Hills Stadium, 97, 99

George Harrison, 4, 22, 28, 29, 34, 37, 52, 65, 71, 80, 81, 94, 101, 110, 115, 116, 120, 129, 130, 135, 147, 149, 152, 157, 163, 171, 173, 177

Hamburg, 41, 42, 44, 45, 46, 47, 53, 54, 61, 140

Help!, 106, 109, 111, 112, 116, 121, 146, 150, 151, 163

India, 42, 146, 163, 166, 167, 172

Indra, 41, 42

Jesus, 23, 39, 141, 142, 143, 144

John Lennon, 4, 7, 10, 19, 23, 25, 27, 32, 33, 35, 62, 64, 70, 76, 80, 82, 84, 94, 115, 116, 117, 119, 135, 136, 138, 141, 142, 147, 149, 150, 153, 160, 166, 174

Larry Kane, 118, 119, 120, 121, 133

Larry Pames, 38

Litherland, 45, 48

Liverpool, 13, 16, 17, 18, 19, 21, 23, 25, 26, 27, 32, 33, 34, 36, 37, 38, 40, 41, 42, 43, 44, 45, 46, 47, 48, 49, 50, 51, 52, 57, 59, 61, 67, 72, 73, 75, 76, 78, 79, 82, 85, 87, 95, 103, 104, 105, 132, 136, 149

Liverpudlian, 34, 136

London, 6, 13, 16, 21, 42, 51, 52, 57, 67, 68, 70, 71, 72, 73, 74, 75, 79, 81, 82, 91, 92, 95, 106, 112, 115, 125, 135, 136, 137, 138, 140, 141, 142, 143, 146, 158, 168

Lord Hariech, 8

LSD, 139, 159, 165, 170

Magical Mystery Tour, 156, 163, 166, 167, 170

Maharishi, 164, 165, 166, 167, 170, 171, 172, 173, 174

Mimi, 20, 36, 37, 66

Molleson, 92, 93

Moondog, 38

mopheads, 15

Neil Aspinall, 10, 45, 47, 55, 68, 74, 81, 101, 117, 129, 134

Neilsen ratings, 83

New York, 6, 7, 9, 16, 42, 84, 85, 92, 93, 96, 97, 99, 112, 113, 122, 124, 125, 128, 133, 141, 144, 157

Norwegian Wood, 146, 152, 155
Palladium, 13, 67, 70, 71, 72, 73, 74, 75, 77, 78
Paperback Writer, 138, 140
Paramount Theater, 96
Paris, 6, 82, 83, 93
Parlophone, 4, 51, 52, 53, 54
Paul McCartney, 4, 7, 9, 22, 23, 32, 33, 35, 45, 47, 62, 76, 80, 81, 111, 114, 115, 119, 162
Pete Shotten, 19
Please Please Me, 54, 75
Quarrymen, 22, 27, 33, 34, 35, 38
Revolver, 140, 144, 156, 160
Richard Goldstein, 157
Ringo Starr, 4, 7, 43, 45, 54, 108, 121
Roll Over Beethoven, 150
Rolling Stones, 110, 125, 134, 164
Royal Variety Show, 67, 80
Schrag, 157, 158
Sgt. Peppers Lonely Hearts Club Band, 156
Shea Stadium, 124, 125, 127, 130, 143
Shenson, 78, 79, 92, 105, 108, 109, 111, 135
Southampton, 32, 81
Telegraph, 77
Transcendental Meditation, 165, 174
Vi Caldwell, 61, 62
Weybridge, 135, 136, 149
When I'm Sixty-Four, 160

Other Titles from Library House Books:

Mystery/Suspense/Thriller/Horror
9781936828517 Witches of Wildwood: Cape May Horror Stories Curran, Mark
Wesley

Cooking
9781936828401 101 Skinny Meals in Minutes: The Fast Weight Loss Cookbook
Abercrombie-Wells, Monique
9781936828340 Italian Cuisine Cookbook: Modern to Classic Easy Recipes For
Busy People Mantini, Sophia
9781936828555 [HC] Nuwave Oven Heavenly Cookbook: Fast Delicious
Recipes for Very Busy People Anderson, A
9781936828548 {HC} Nuwave Oven Cookbook: 101 Delicious Recipes for the
Countertop Connoisseur Benedict,L
9781936828203 The Crock Pot Connoisseur: Delicious Slow Cooker Recipes
For (Very) Busy People Paulson, Peggy
9781936828395 215 Delicious and Appetizing Classic Soup Recipes for
Modern Kitchens Turner, Lisa
9781936828388 Delicious Pennsylvania Dutch Cooking: 172 Traditional
Proven Recipes for the Modern Kitchen

Biography/History
9781936828593 Alexander Hamilton: The True and Romantic Story of
America's Greatest Statesman - Gertrude Atherton –
9781936828043 The Papers and Writings of Abraham Lincoln Volume One:
Special Constitutional Collectors Edition
9781936828104 Papers Of Thomas Jefferson: A Collection of Selected
Writings, Memoirs and Letters Jefferson, Thomas
9780970677389 The Federalist Papers: America's Greatest Living
Documents Madison, James
9781936828616 - The Beatles! The Inside Story Behind the World's Greatest
Rock and Roll Band - Kerry Kensington
978-1-936828-60-9 - Ulysses S. Grant: His Life and Times - A Biography –
Grant, Ulysses – Library Collectors Ed.

Self Help/Business
9781936828319 Social Media Marketing: Mastering The Power of Online
Networking Powers, Daniel
9781936828364 Crowdfunding with Kickstarter: A Beginner's Guide to
Crowdfunding Success
9781936828265 The Art of Public Speaking - Millenium Edition Carnegie, Dale
9781936828180 Voice Training: A Primer For Better Speaking and
Singing Hendrix, PH.D Marlo

Self Help/Psychology
9781936828142 Happiness: Finding Inner Peace and Contentment Through Mind Awareness/Relaxation Vishnu,G
9781936828135 Ancient Wisdom - Modern World Advice For Better Living Vishnu, PH.D. Gopi
9780970677396 How to Meditate: Eliminating Stress and Worry Through Relaxation and Meditation Chopra, S. Williams
9781936828470 The Road to Love: Zen Meditation Practice For Beginners Tchogen, Roshi
9781936828418 The Zen Experience Hoover, Thomas
9781936828531 {HC} Tao Te Ching (the Way) by Lao-Tzu: Special Collector's Edition

Self Help/Writing
9781936828166 Writing From Within: Tapping The Creative Unconscious: How to Use Your Subconscious Mind To Supercharge Your Creative Writing Curran, Mark W.
9781936828449 How To Write A Book: Writing A Novel That Sells Brown, Dan

Nutrition/Diet
9780970677372 Living Thin In A Fast Food World: How To Lose Weight & Stay That Way Bennett, Jill Anne

Self Help/Music Business
9781936828180 Voice Training: A Primer For Better Speaking and Singing Hendrix, PH.D Marlo
9781936828173 Sing! Learn How To Sing Like An Idol: Vocal Techniques For Modern Singers Curran, Mark W.
9780970677365 Sell Your Music : How To Profitably Sell Your Own Recordings Online Curran, Mark W
9780970677327 Getting Gigs! the Musician's and Singer's Survival Guide to Booking Better Paying Jobs Curran, Mark W.

Literature/Classics
9781936828463 The Scarlet Letter: A Romance Hawthorne, Nathaniel
9781936828524 [HC} Plato's the Republic: Special Collector's Edition Plato
9781936828067 {SC} Plato's The Republic: Special Collector's Edition Plato
9781936828050 The Adventures of Sherlock Holmes: Special Collectors Edition: Doyle, Arthur Conan
9781936828036 Leaves Of Grass: Unabridged Special Collectors Edition Whitman, Walt
9781936828012 Adventures of Tom Sawyer Special Literary Collectors Edition with a Preface by Mark Twain Twain, Mark
9781936828029 Adventures of Huckleberry Finn: Special Collectors Edition with Forward by H.L. Menken
9780970677341 The Raven: The Selected Poems of Edgar Allan Poe - Special Collector's Edition

9781936828371 Grimms' Fairy Tales by the Brothers Grimm Grimm, Jacob Ludwig Carl
9781936828302 Alice's Adventures in Wonderland Carroll, Lewis
9781936828296 Siddhartha: An Indian Tale Hesse, Hermann
9781936828289 Macbeth Shakespeare, William
9781936828272 Pride and Prejudice - New Millenium Edition Austen, Jane
9781936828210 Frankenstein - Mary Wollstonecraft Shelley - Special Collector's Edition
9781936828159 Dracula: Complete Unabridged Collectors Edition with Preface by Stephen King - Bram Stoker
9781936828111 Anthem: Special Annotated Collectors Edition with a Foreward by Ayn Rand - Ayn Rand
9781936828098 On the Origin of Species: Special Collector's Edition - Charles Darwin

Human Sexuality
9781936828005 The Kama Sutra of Vatsyayana: Ancient Explorations Into Eroticism For the Modern Age Vatsyayana

Film/Drama/Self-Help/Acting
9780970677334 Scenes That Sizzle!: Contemporary Dramatic Monologues for Actors Brylsteen, Joshua Brylsteen
9781936828579 The Total Film-Maker: The New Collectors Edition Lewis, Jerry

Travel Guides/Photography
9781936828586 [Case Laminate] Hidden Hawaii - In Search Of The Lost Islands Mark, Curran Wesley

DVD
Abandoned Dead - Movie - Suspense/Mystery/Thriller - [DVD, DIGITAL DOWNLOAD)
Poe: In His Own Words: An Evening With Edgar Allan Poe - Educational/ Documentary/Filmed Stage Play - [DVD, DIGITAL DOWNLOAD)

www.libraryhousebooks.com

Special 20% Discounts to Bookstores and Libraries